Easy Piano

HALLELUJAH, IMAGINE,
& Other SONGS OF
INSPIRATION

ISBN 978-1-70513-102-2

Visit Hal Leonard Online at
www.halleonard.com

Contact us:
Hal Leonard
7777 West Bluemound Road
Milwaukee, WI 53213
Email: info@halleonard.com

In Europe, contact:
Hal Leonard Europe Limited
42 Wigmore Street
Marylebone, London, W1U 2RN
Email: info@halleonardeurope.com

In Australia, contact:
Hal Leonard Australia Pty. Ltd.
4 Lentara Court
Cheltenham, Victoria, 3192 Australia
Email: info@halleonard.com.au

CONTENTS

ANYWAY

Words and Music by BRAD WARREN,
BRETT WARREN and MARTINA McBRIDE

Moderate Ballad

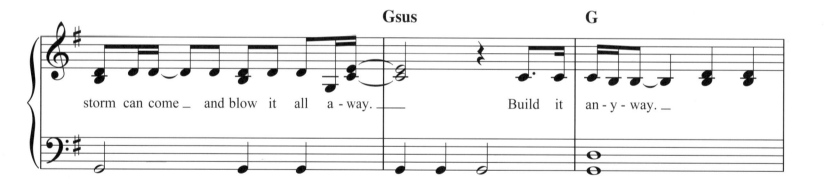

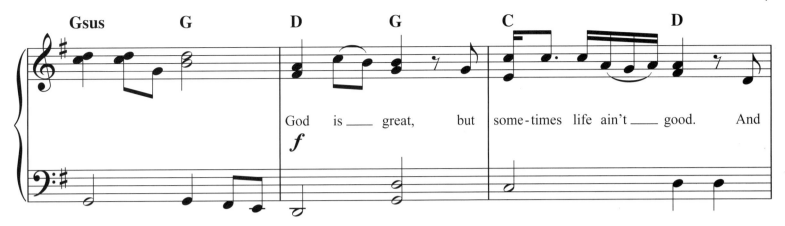

God is ___ great, but some-times life ain't ___ good. And

when I ___ pray, it does-n't al-ways turn out like I think it should, but I do it

an - y - way. ___ Yeah, I do it an - y - way, ___ yeah. ___

You can   pour   your   soul ___   out   sing - ing

a   song   you   be - lieve ___   in   that   to - mor - row   they'll ___   for - get   you   ev - er

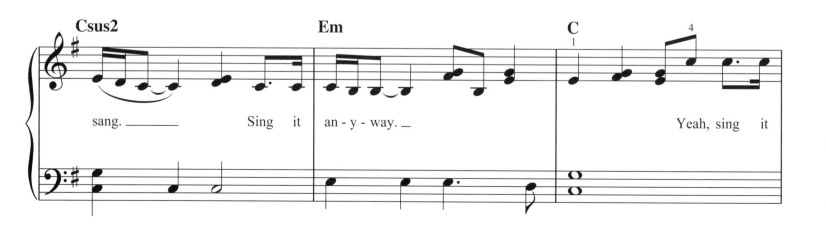

sang. _____   Sing   it   an - y - way. ___   Yeah, sing   it

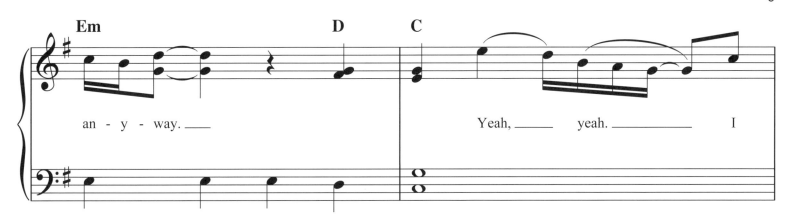

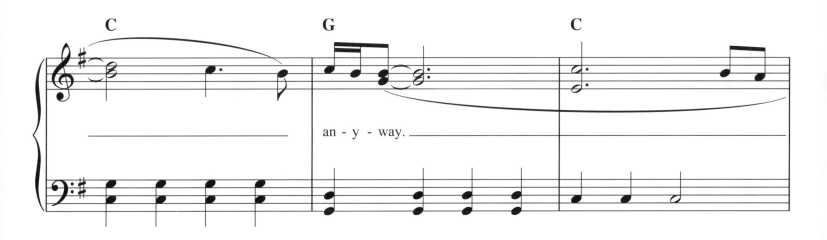

BEAUTIFUL

Words and Music by
LINDA PERRY

Moderately slow

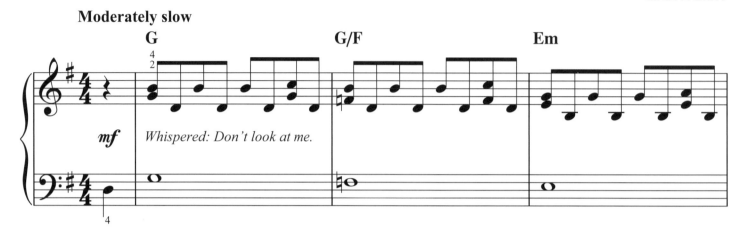

Whispered: Don't look at me.

Ev-'ry day is so
To all your friends you're de-

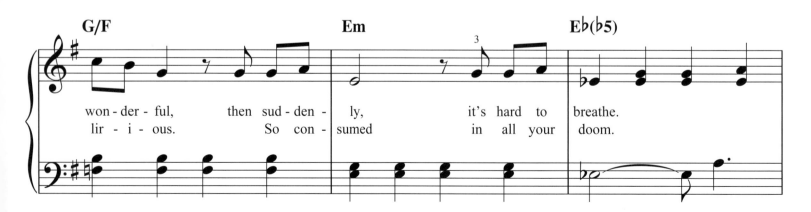

won-der-ful, then sud-den-ly, it's hard to breathe.
lir-i-ous. So con-sumed in all your doom.

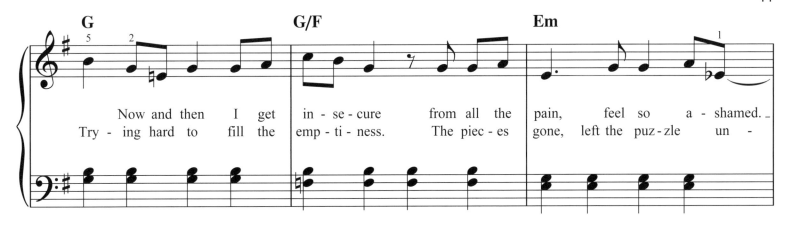

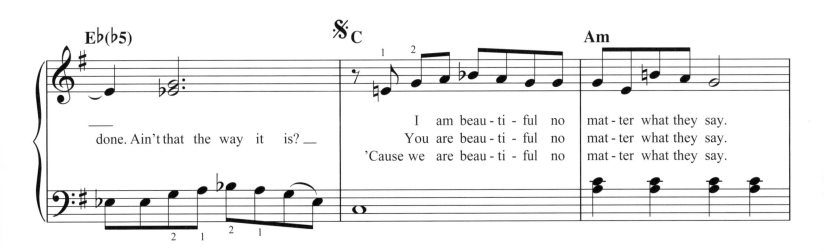

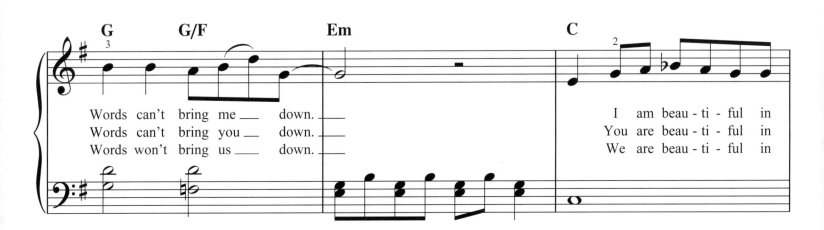

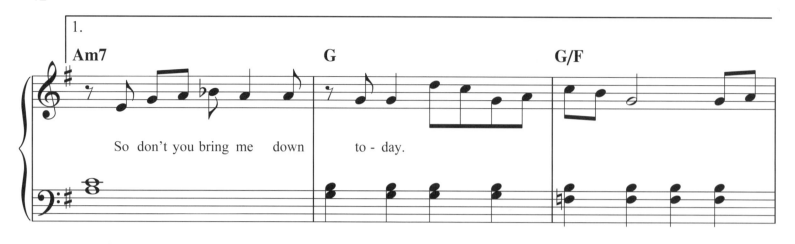

So don't you bring me down to - day.

So don't you bring me down to -

day. No mat - ter what we do. No mat - ter what we say. We're the song in - side the

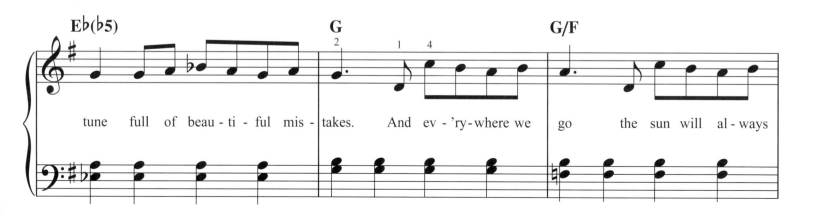

tune full of beau - ti - ful mis - takes. And ev - 'ry-where we go the sun will al - ways

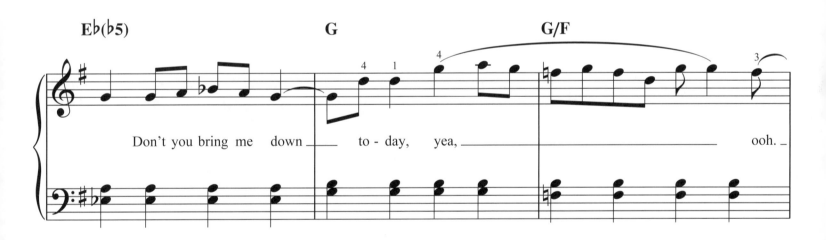

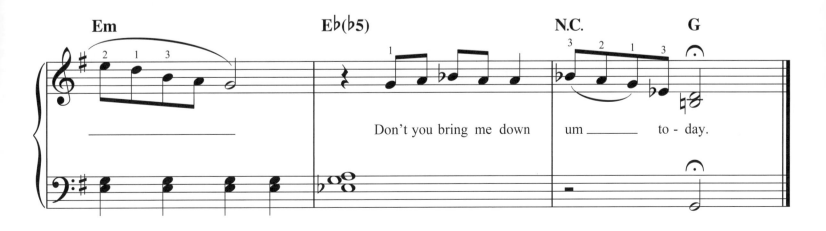

BEAUTIFUL DAY

Words by BONO
Music by U2

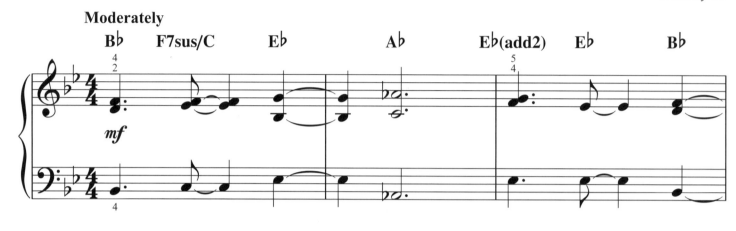

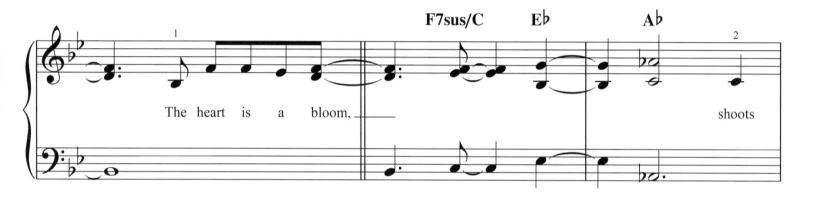

The heart is a bloom, ___ shoots

up through the ston-y ground. ___ But there's no room, ___

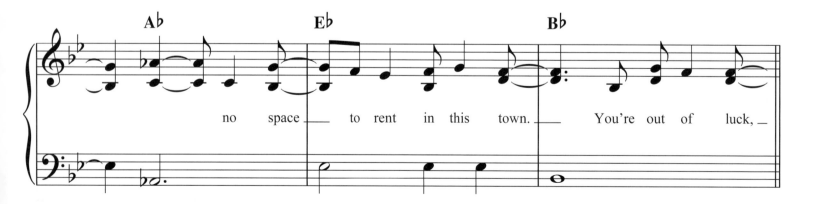

no space ___ to rent in this town. ___ You're out of luck, ___

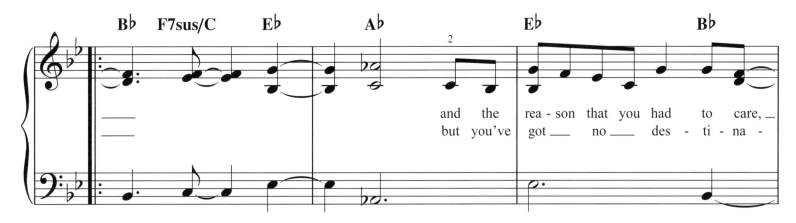

and the rea - son that you had to care, __
but you've got __ no __ des - ti - na -

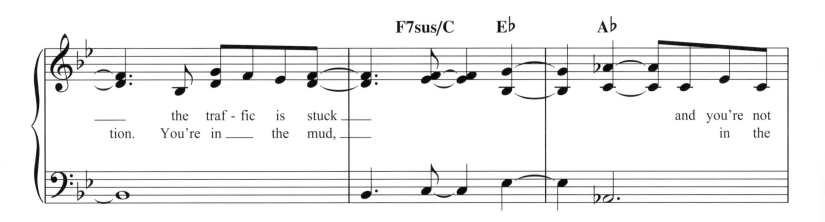

__ the traf - fic is stuck __
tion. You're in __ the mud, __

and you're not
in the

mov - in' an - y - where. __ You thought you'd found __ a friend __
maze of her i - mag - i - na - tion. You love this town, __

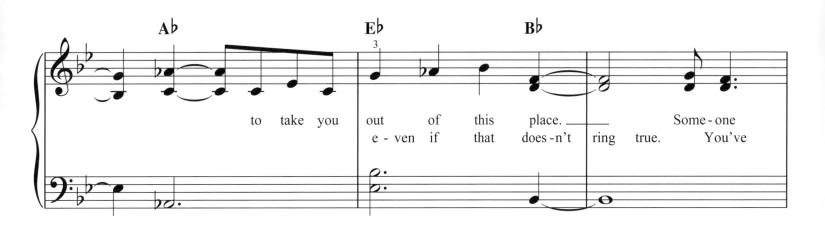

to take you out of this place. __ Some - one
e - ven if that does - n't ring true. You've

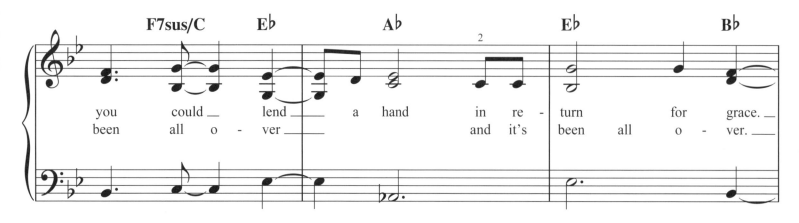

you could ___ lend ___ a hand in re - turn for grace. ___
been all o - ver ___ and it's been all o - ver. ___

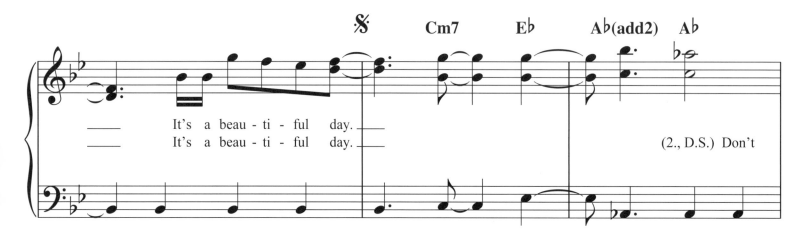

___ It's a beau - ti - ful day. ___
___ It's a beau - ti - ful day. ___

(2., D.S.) Don't

The sky falls, you feel ___ like it's a beau - ti - ful day. ___ }
let it get a - way. ___ A beau - ti - ful day. ___ }

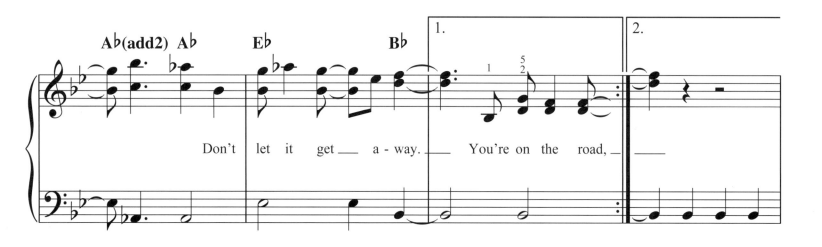

Don't let it get ___ a - way. ___ You're on the road, ___ ___

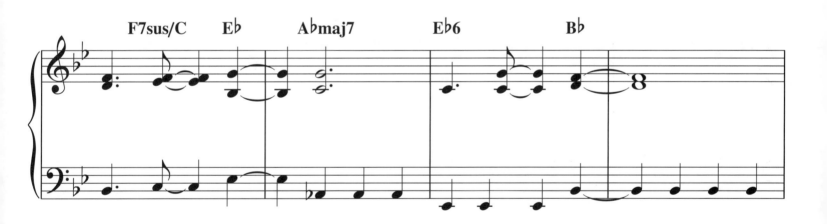

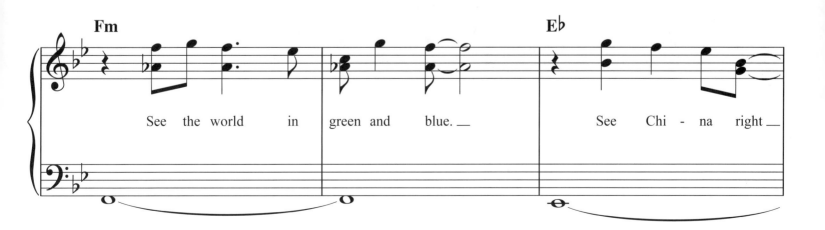

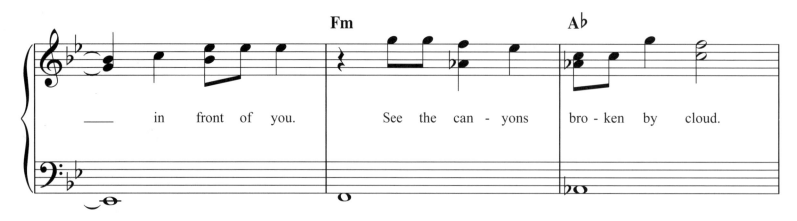

_____ in front of you.   See the can - yons   bro - ken by   cloud.

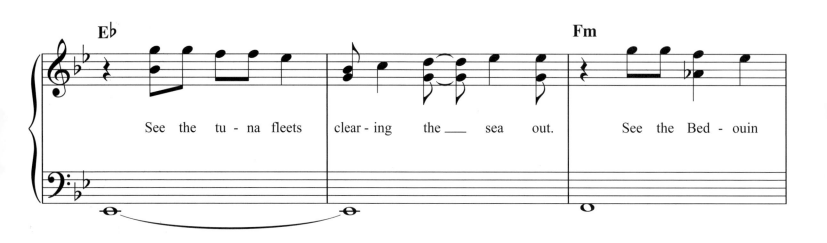

See the tu - na fleets   clear - ing the ___ sea out.   See the Bed - ouin

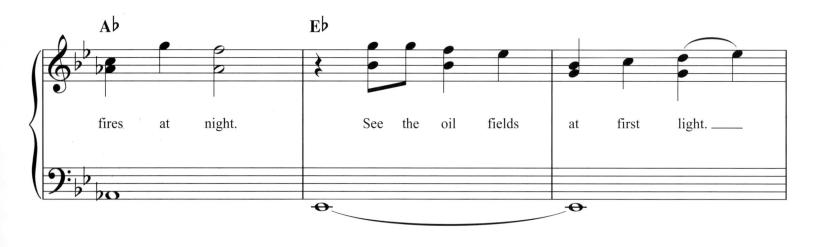

fires   at   night.   See the oil fields   at   first   light. ____

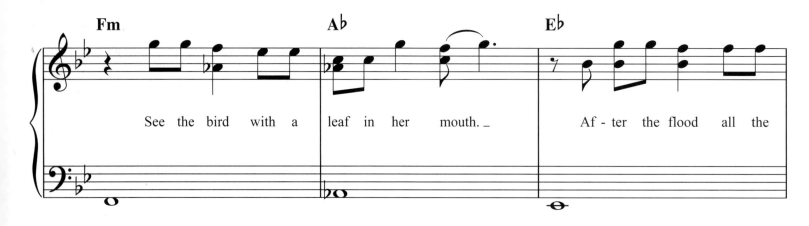

See the bird   with a   leaf in her   mouth. _   Af - ter the flood   all the

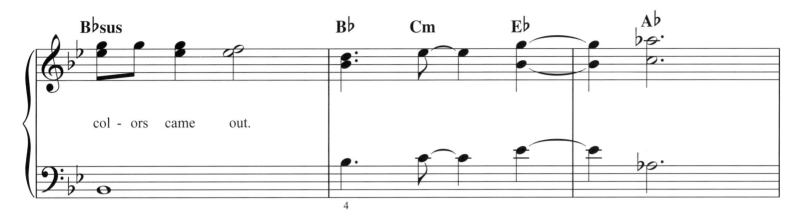

col - ors came out.

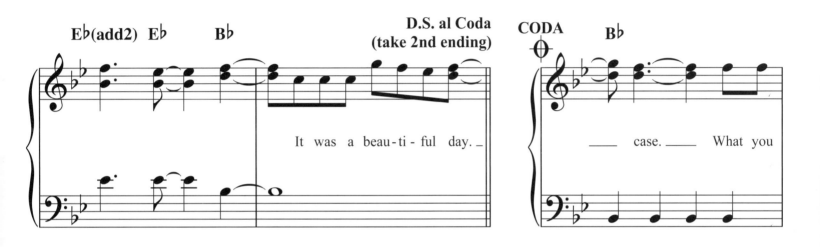

D.S. al Coda
(take 2nd ending)

CODA

E♭(add2) E♭   B♭   B♭

It was a beau-ti-ful day. ___   ___ case. ___ What you

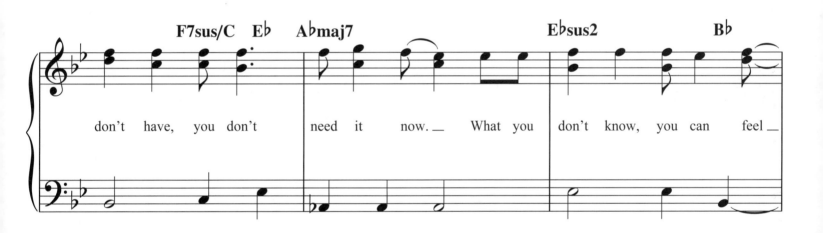

F7sus/C E♭   A♭maj7   E♭sus2   B♭

don't have, you don't   need it now. ___ What you   don't know, you can feel ___

F7sus/C E♭   A♭maj7

___ it some-how. What you   don't have, you don't ___   need it now. ___ You don't

need it now. _____ It's a beau - ti - ful day.

rit.

DON'T STOP BELIEVIN'

Words and Music by STEVE PERRY,
NEAL SCHON and JONATHAN CAIN

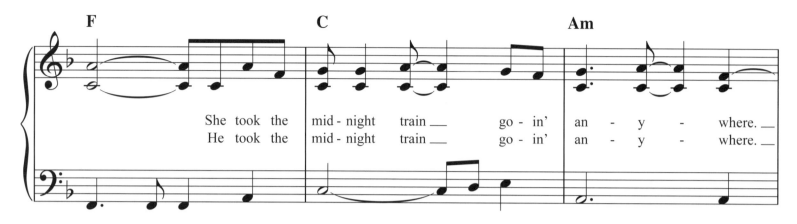

She took the mid-night train ___ go-in' an-y - where. ___
He took the mid-night train ___ go-in' an-y - where. ___

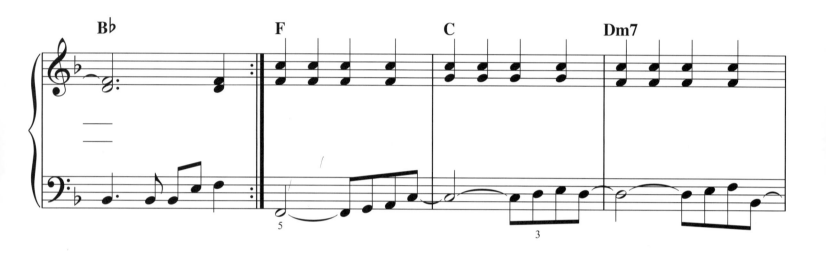

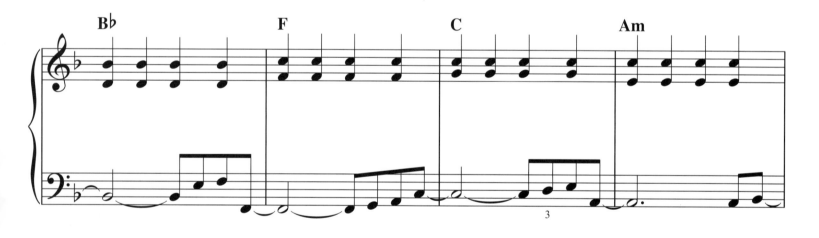

A sing-er in a smok-y room. ___

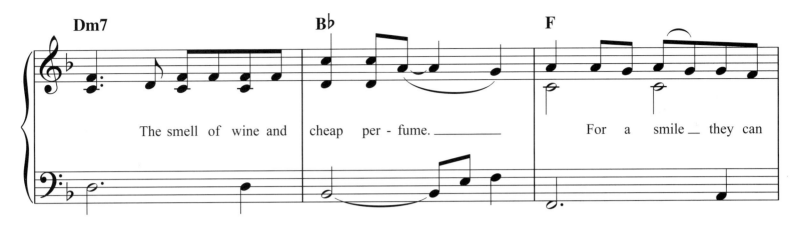

The smell of wine and cheap per - fume. ____ For a smile ____ they can

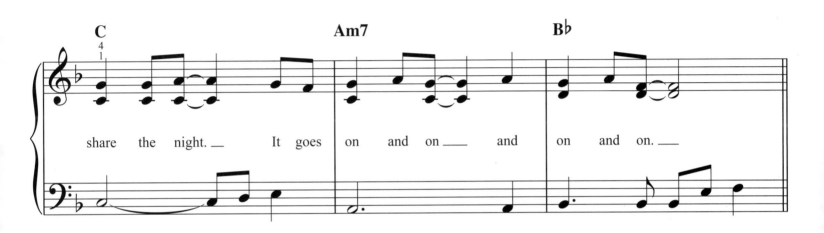

share the night. ____ It goes on and on ____ and on and on. ____

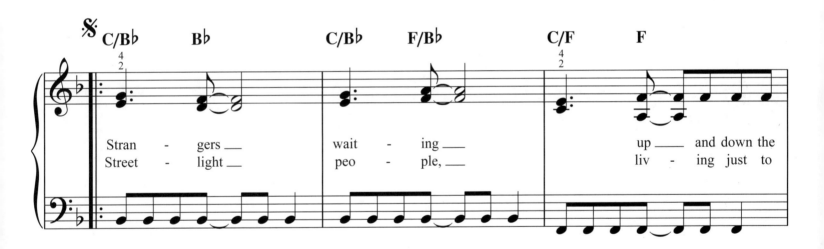

Stran - gers ____ wait - ing ____ up ____ and down the
Street - light ____ peo - ple, ____ liv - ing just to

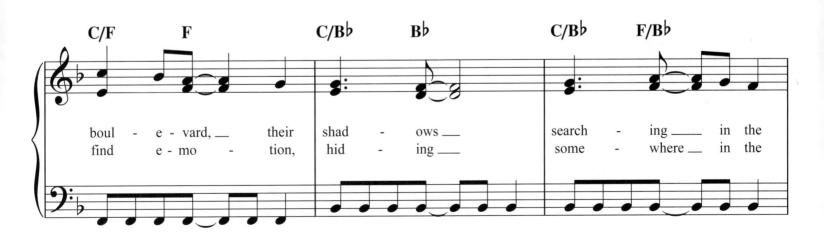

boul - e - vard, ____ their shad - ows ____ search - ing ____ in the
find e - mo - tion, hid - ing ____ some - where ____ in the

BELIEVE

Words and Music by ELTON JOHN
and BERNIE TAUPIN

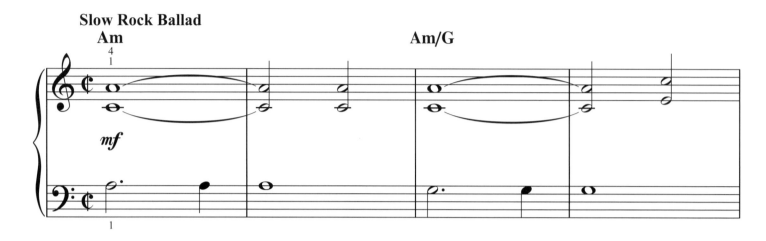

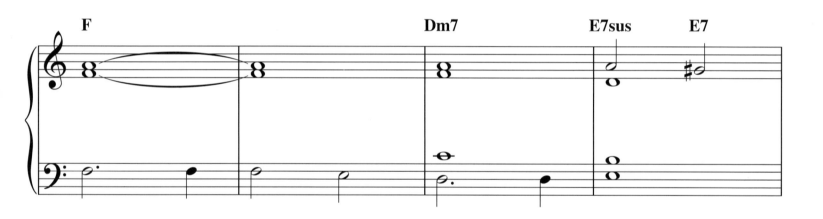

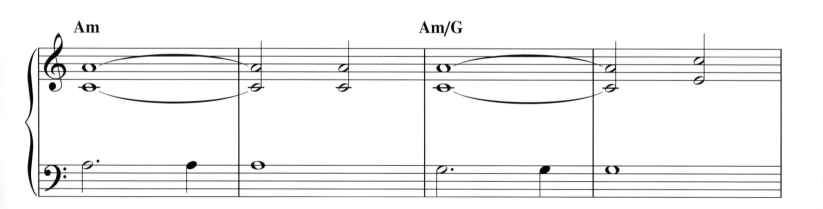

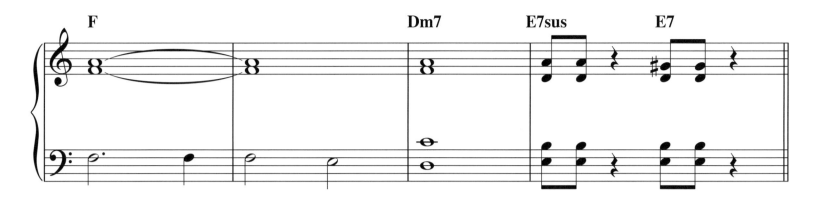

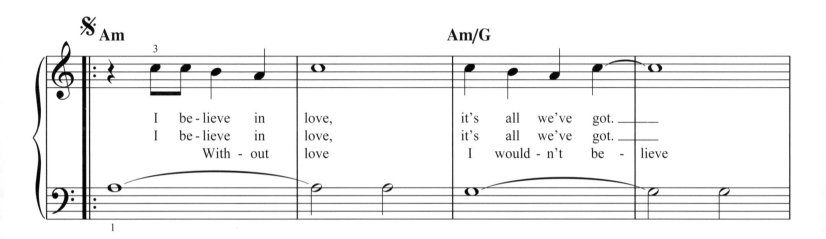

I be-lieve in love, it's all we've got.
I be-lieve in love, it's all we've got.
With - out love I would - n't be - lieve

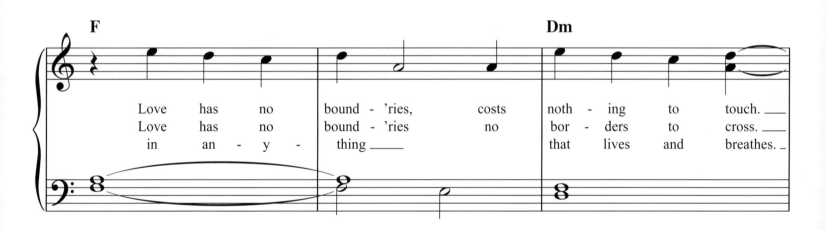

Love has no bound - 'ries, costs noth - ing to touch.
Love has no bound - 'ries no bor - ders to cross.
in an - y - thing that lives and breathes.

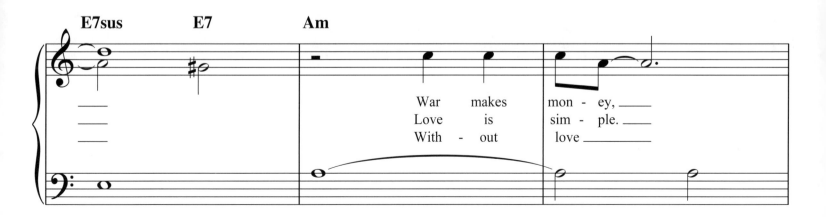

War makes mon - ey,
Love is sim - ple.
With - out love

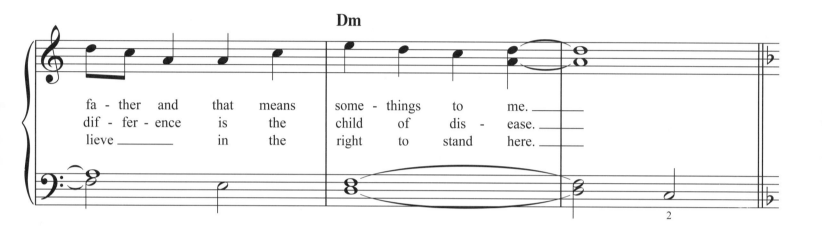

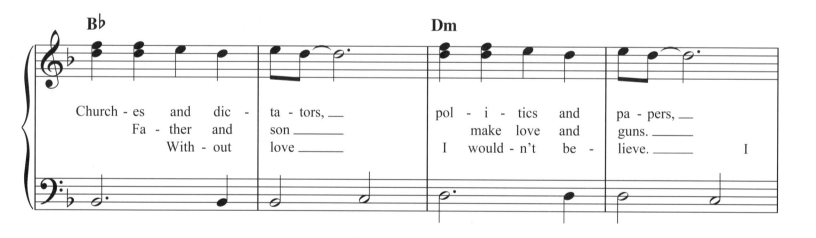

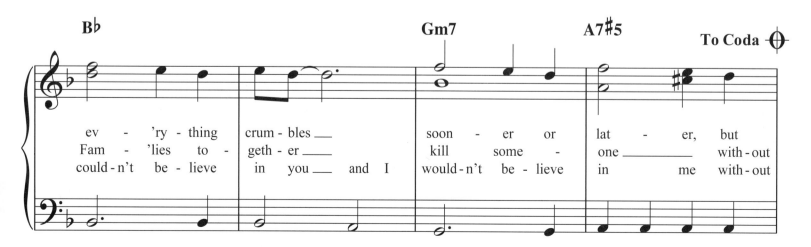

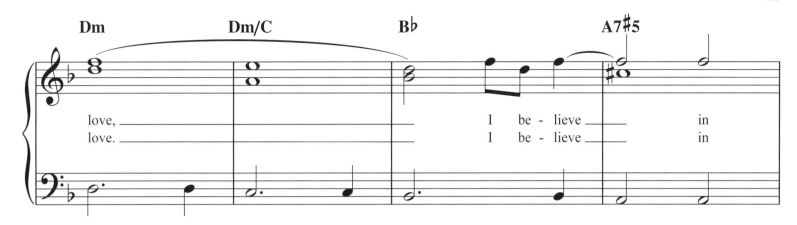

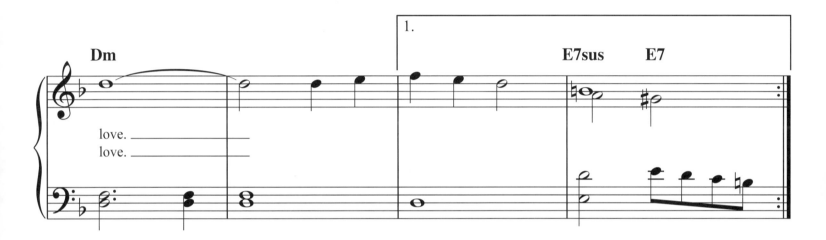

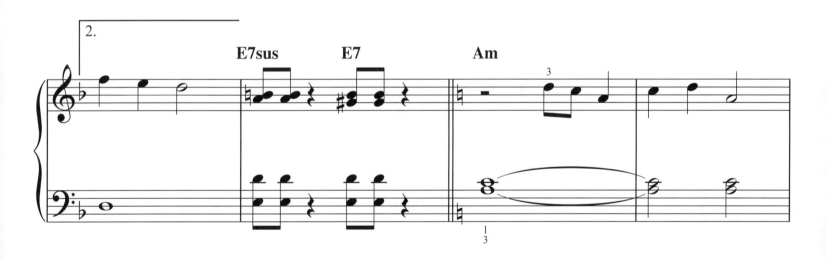

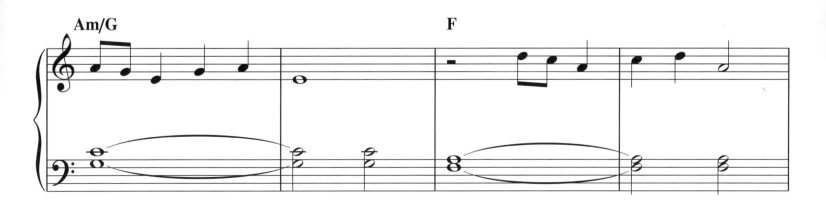

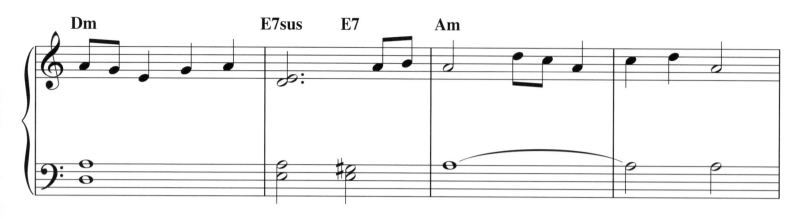

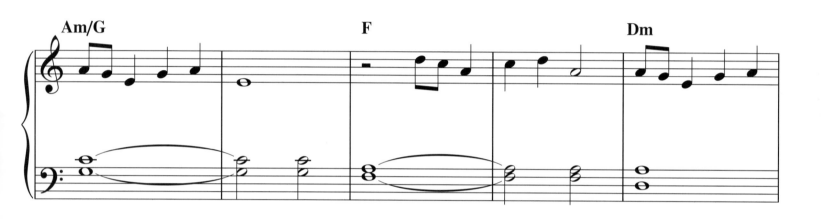

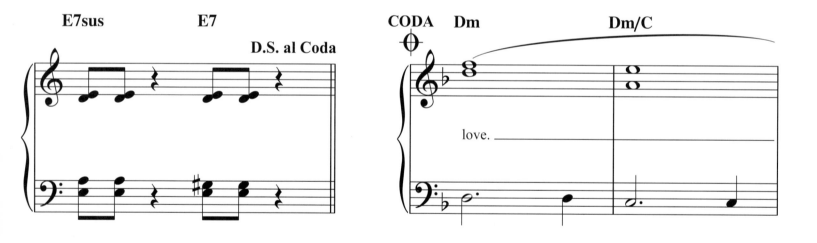

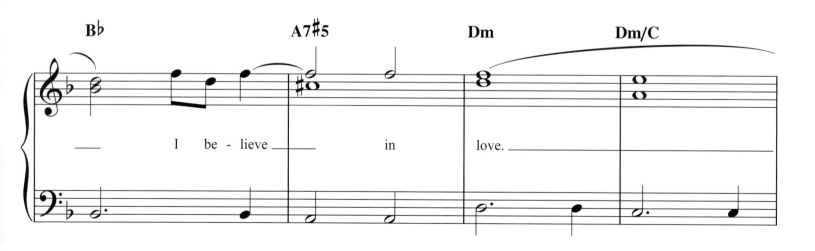

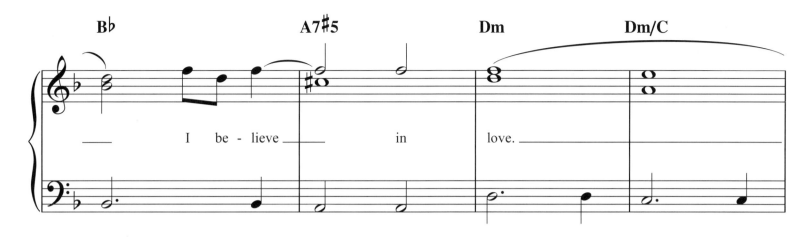

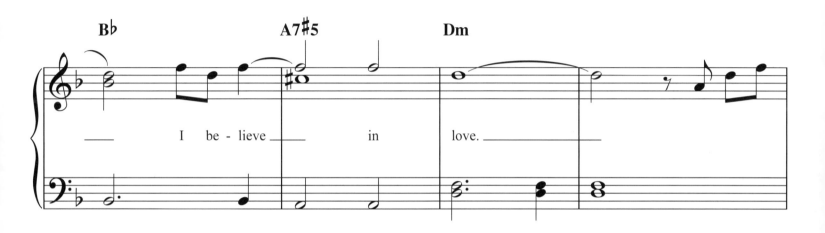

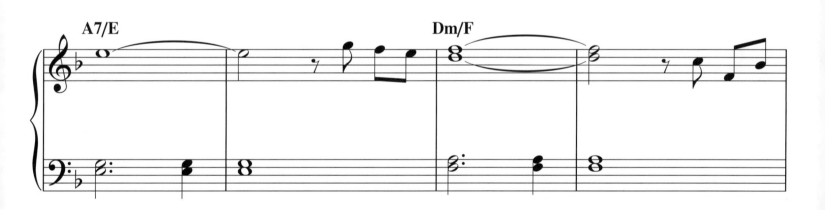

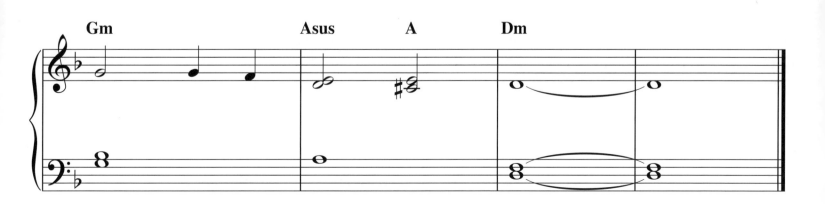

CIRCLE OF LIFE
from THE LION KING

Music by ELTON JOHN
Lyrics by TIM RICE

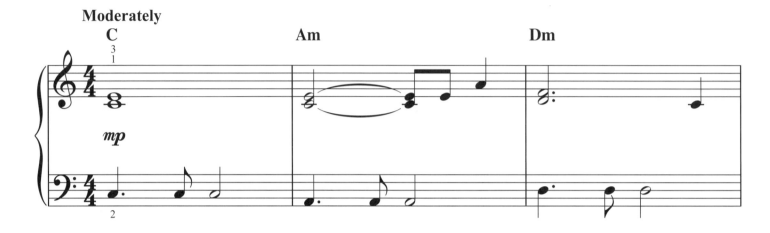

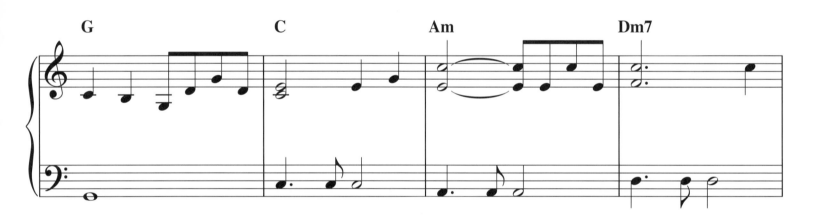

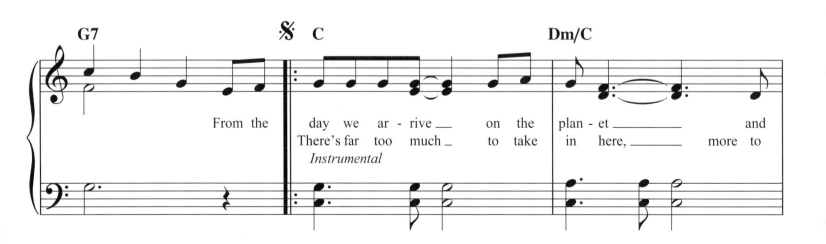

From the | day we ar-rive __ on the | plan-et _____ and
There's far too much _ to take | in here, _____ more to
Instrumental

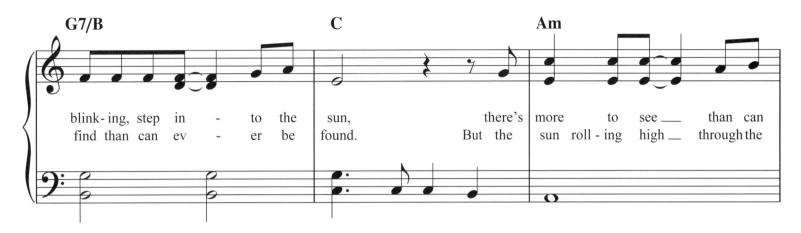

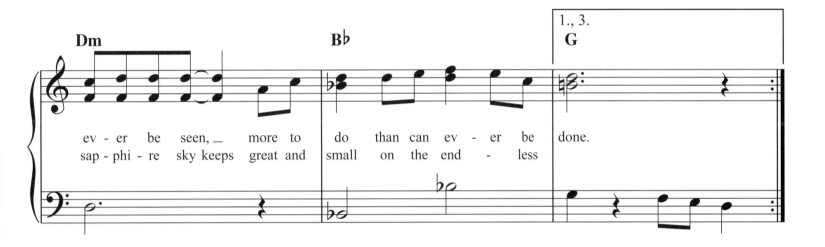

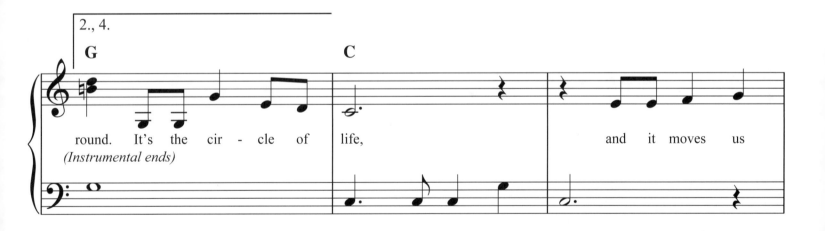

34

through faith and ___ love,

'til we find our

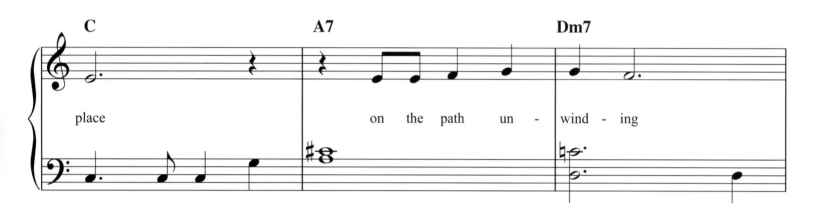

place

on the path un - wind - ing

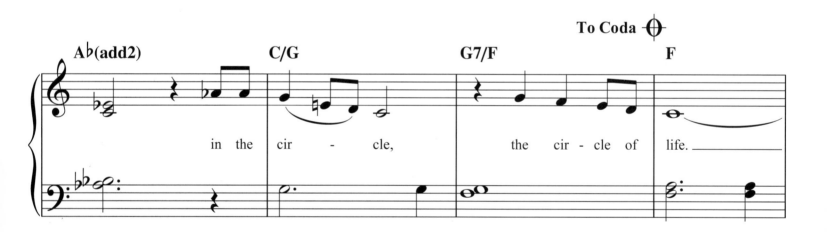

To Coda

in the cir - cle,

the cir - cle of life. ___

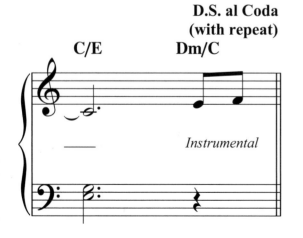

D.S. al Coda
(with repeat)

___

Instrumental

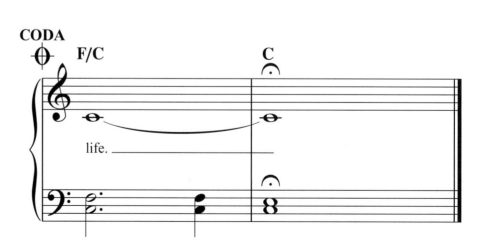

CODA

life. ___

HERO

Words and Music by MARIAH CAREY
and WALTER AFANASIEFF

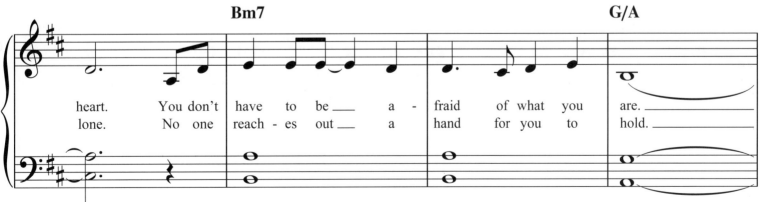

There's a he — ro if you look in-side your heart. You don't have to be a - fraid of what you are.

long road when you face the world a - lone. No one reach - es out a hand for you to hold.

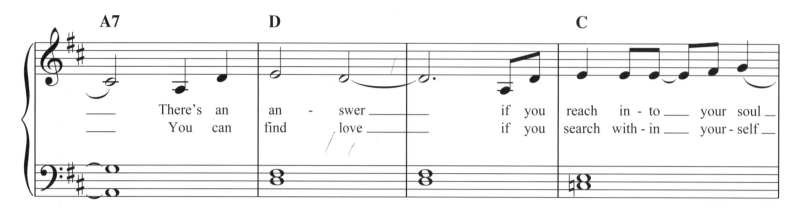

There's an an - swer _____ if you reach in - to _____ your soul _____
You can find love _____ if you search with - in _____ your - self _____

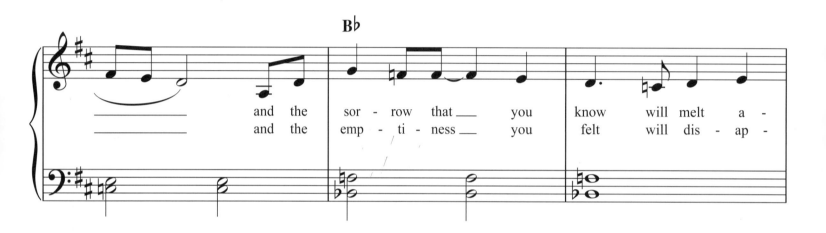

and the sor - row that _____ you know will melt a -
and the emp - ti - ness _____ you felt will dis - ap -

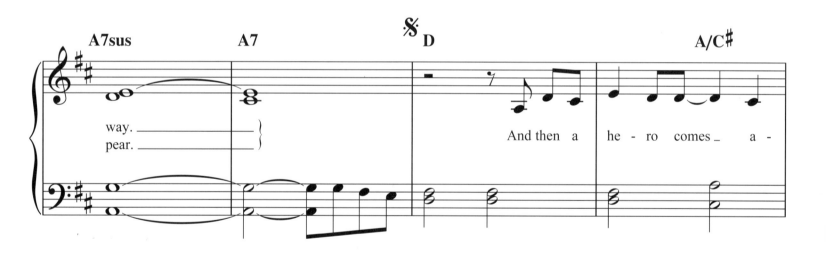

way. _____
pear. _____

And then a he - ro comes _____ a -

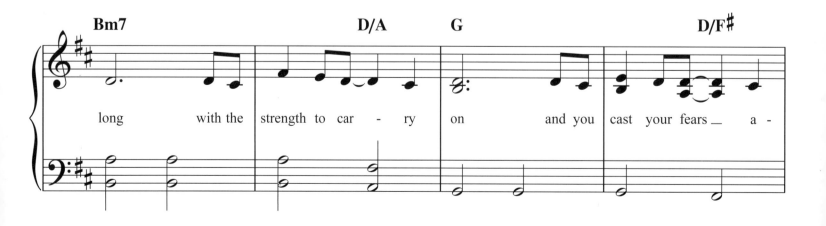

long with the strength to car - ry on and you cast your fears _____ a -

side, and you know you can ___ sur - vive. So when you

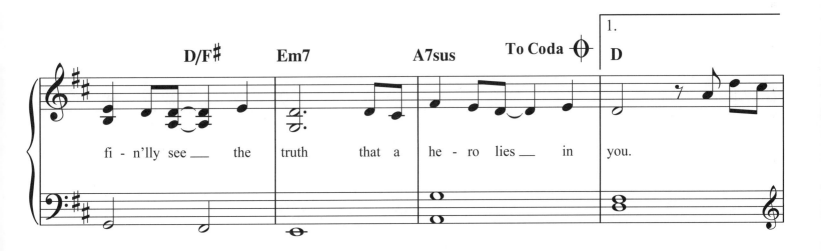

feel like hope ___ is gone look in - side you and ___ be strong and you'll

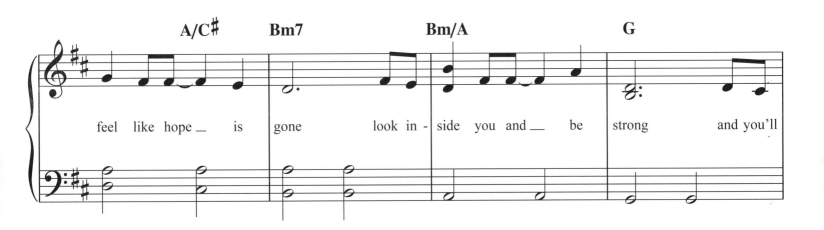

fi - n'lly see ___ the truth that a he - ro lies ___ in you.

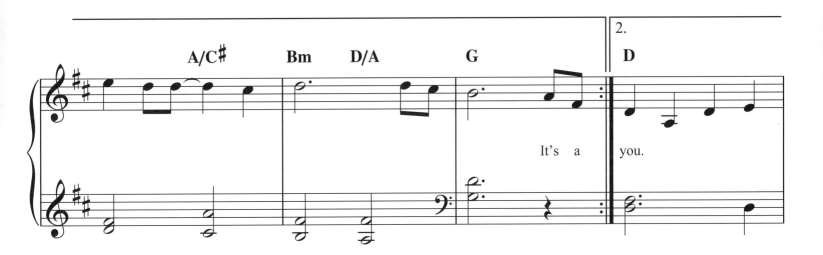

It's a you.

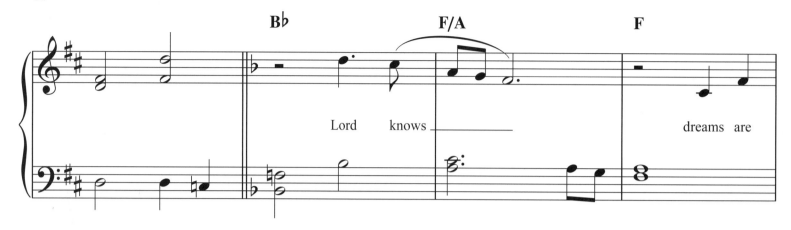

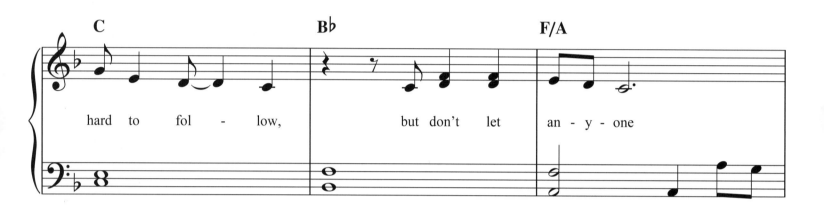

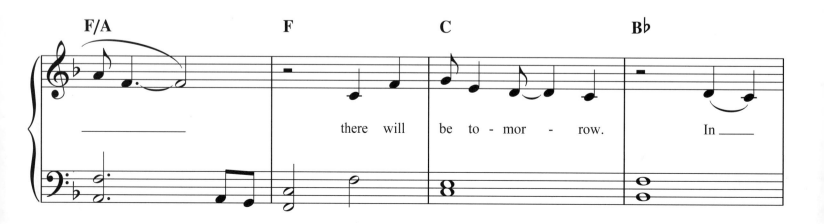

D.S. al Coda

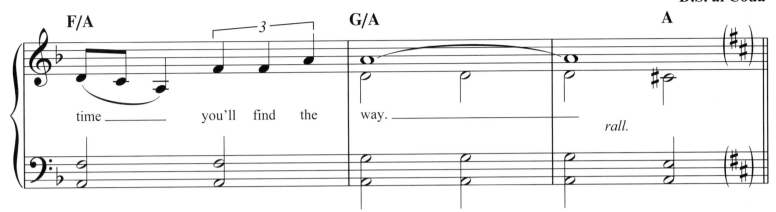

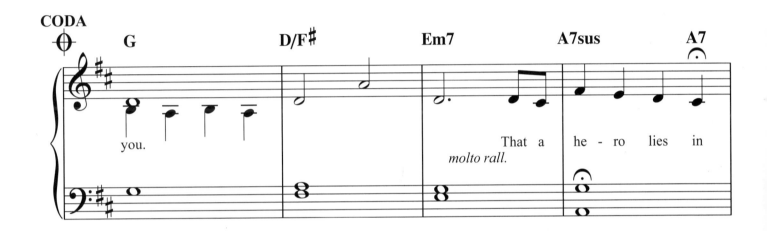

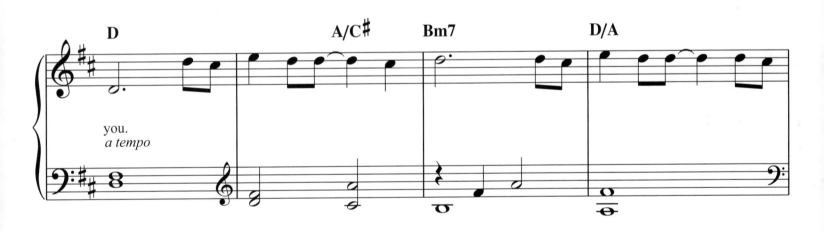

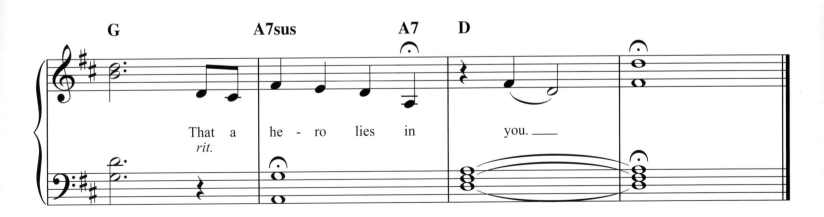

THE CLIMB

from HANNAH MONTANA: THE MOVIE

Words and Music by JESSI ALEXANDER
and JON MABE

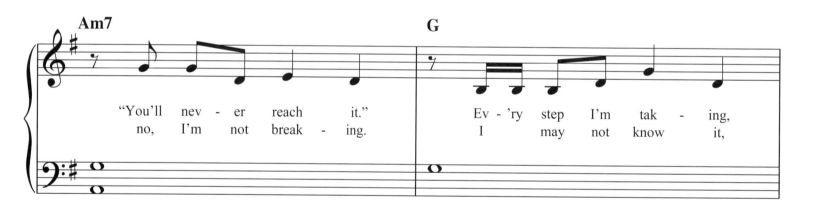

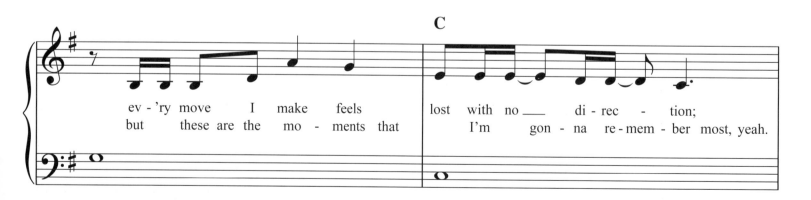

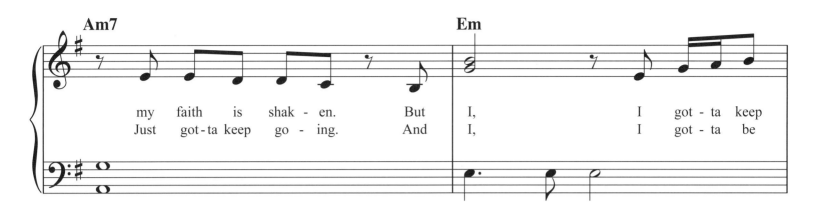

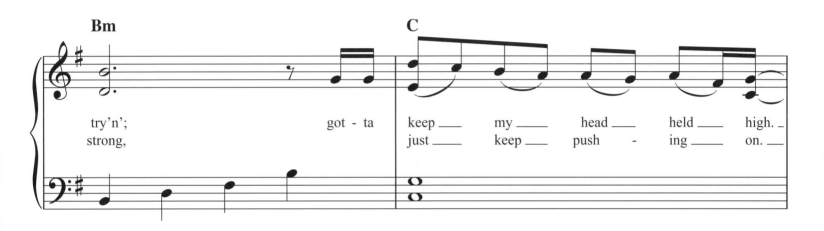

There's al-ways gon-na be an-oth - er moun - tain; __

I'm al-ways gon-na wan-na make __ it move.

Al-ways gon-na be an up - hill bat - tle;

some-bod-y's gon-na have to lose. Ain't a-bout how fast I get there;

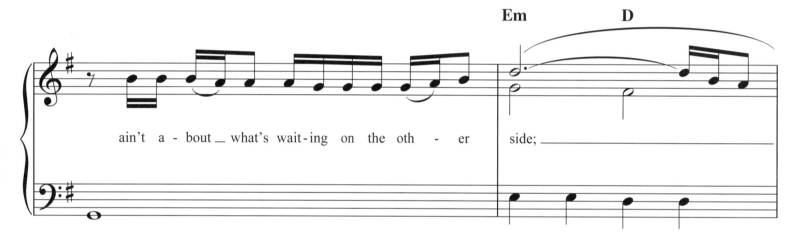

ain't a-bout what's wait-ing on the oth - er side;

it's the climb.

Keep on

mov - ing, keep climb - ing; keep _____ the faith, _____ ba - by. _____

It's all _____ a - bout, _____ it's all _____ a - bout _____ the climb. _____

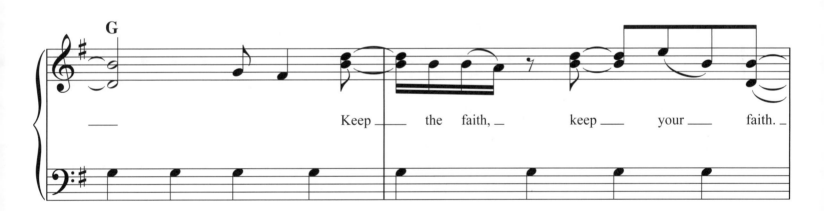

Keep _____ the faith, _____ keep _____ your _____ faith. _____

EYE OF THE TIGER
Theme from ROCKY III

Words and Music by FRANK SULLIVAN
and JIM PETERIK

lyrics:

1. Ris- in' up back on the street, _____ did my time, took my
2. So man - y times it hap-pens too fast. _____ You trade your pas - sion for
3.-4. *(See additional lyrics)*

chanc - es. Went the dis - tance. Now I'm back on my feet, just a
glo - ry. Don't lose your grip _____ on the dreams of the past. You must

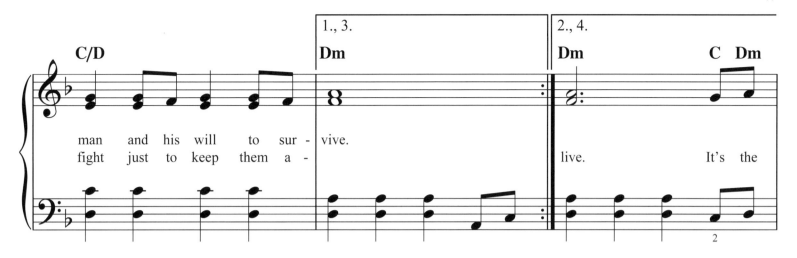

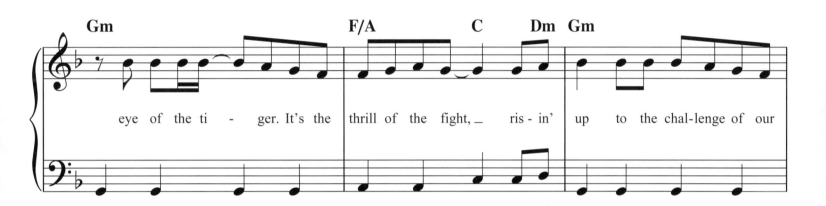

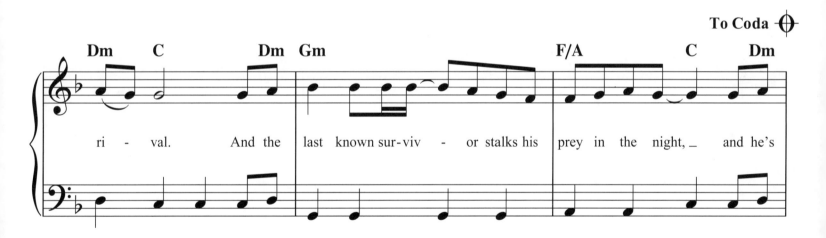

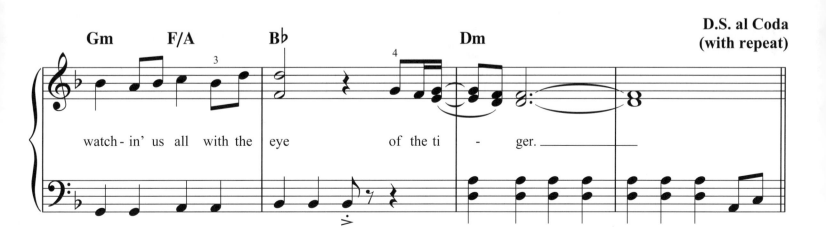

48

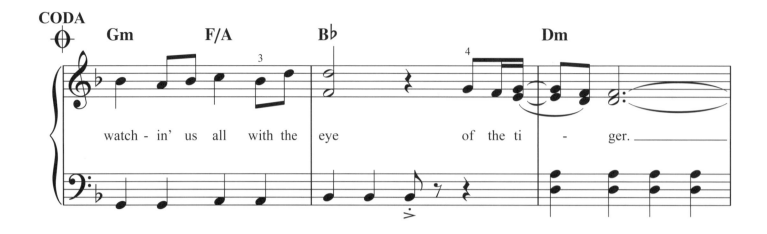

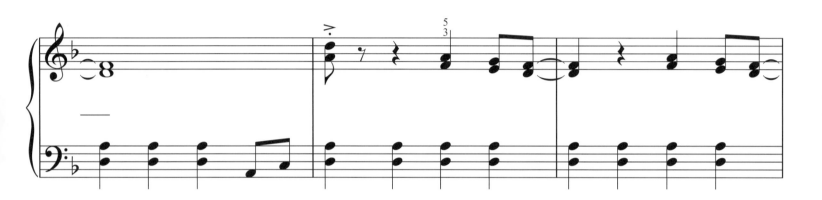

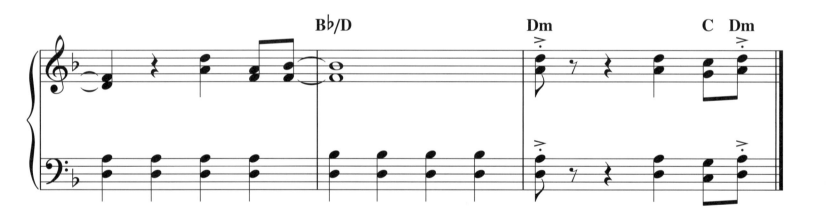

Additional Lyrics

3. Face to face, out in the heat,
   Hangin' tough, stayin' hungry.
   They stack the odds, still we take to the street
   For the kill with the skill to survive.

4. Risin' up, straight to the top.
   Had the guts, got the glory.
   Went the distance. Now I'm not gonna stop,
   Just a man and his will to survive.

MUSIC OF MY HEART

Words and Music by
DIANE WARREN

You'll nev - er know _____ what you've done for me, _____ what your
You were the one _____ al - ways on my side, _____ al - ways

faith in me _____ has done for my _____ soul. _____
stand - ing by, _____ see - ing me _____ through. _____

You'll nev - er know _____ the gift _____ you've giv - en me; _____ I'll car - ry
You were the song _____ that al - ways made me sing; _____ I'm sing - ing this

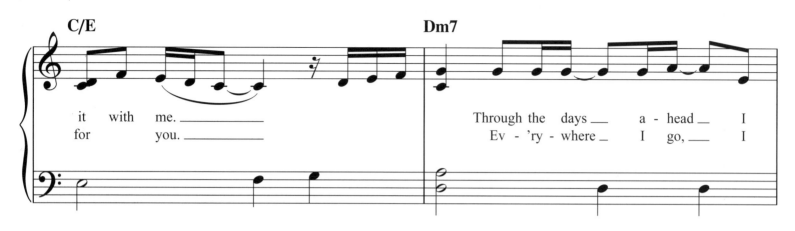

it with me. _____
for you. _____
Through the days ___ a - head ___ I
Ev - 'ry - where ___ I go, ___ I

think of days ___ be - fore, when you made me
think of where ___ I've been and of the
hope for some - thing bet - ter and made me
one who knew ___ me bet - ter than an - y - one

reach for some - thing more. ___
ev - er will ___ a - gain. ___
You taught me to run, ___ you taught me to fly, ___ helped me to free ___

___ the me ___ in - side, _____ helped me hear the
mu - sic of ___ my heart, helped me hear the

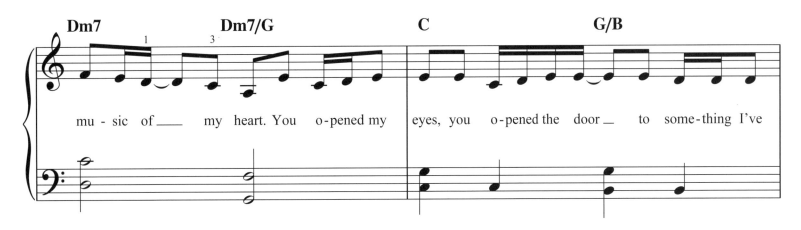

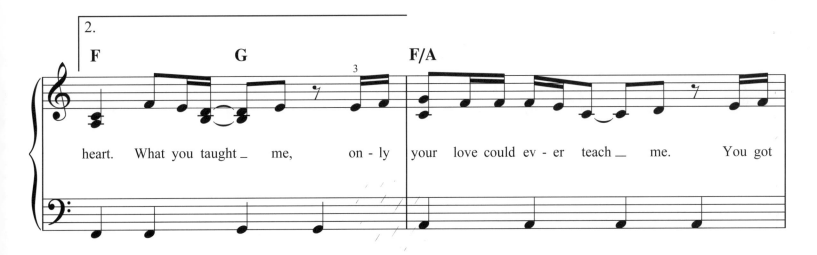

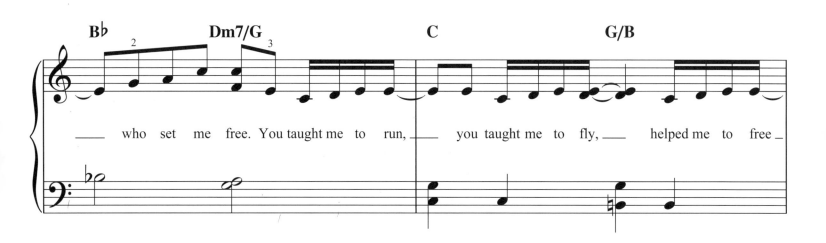

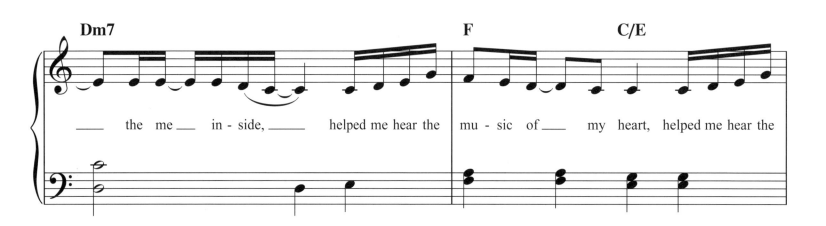

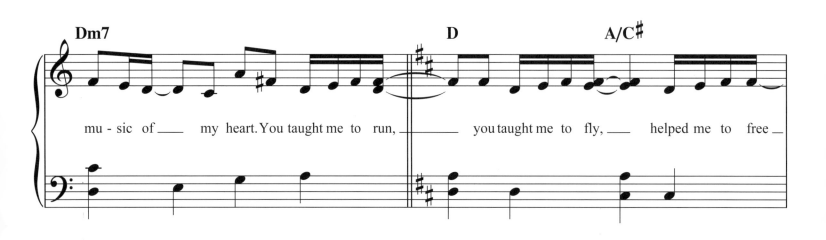

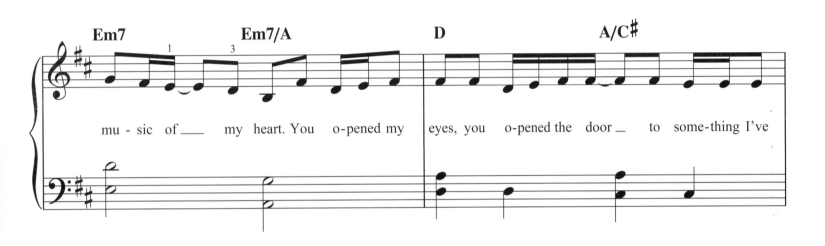

HALLELUJAH

Words and Music by
LEONARD COHEN

Moderately slow, in 2

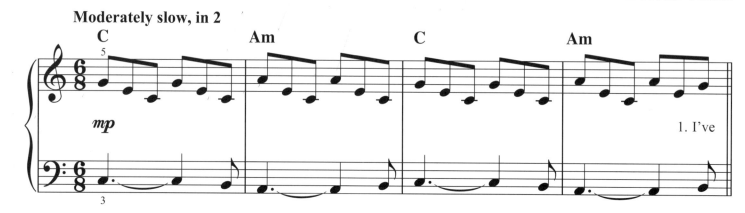

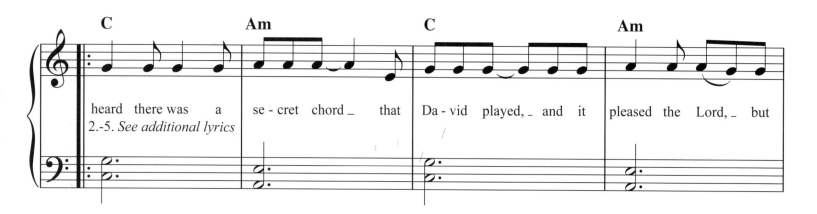

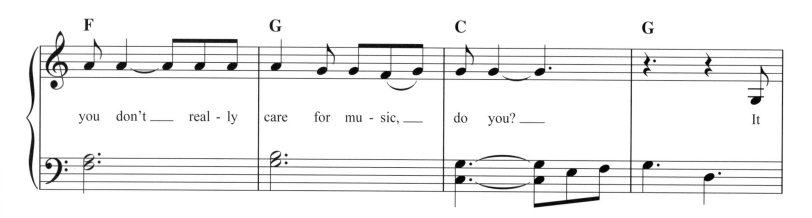

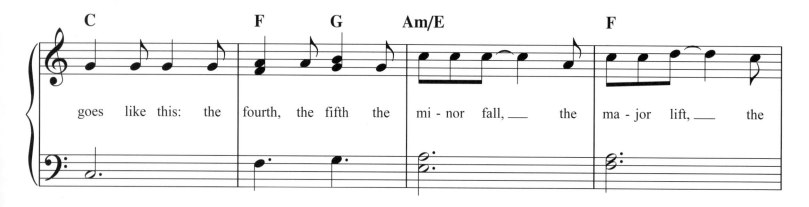

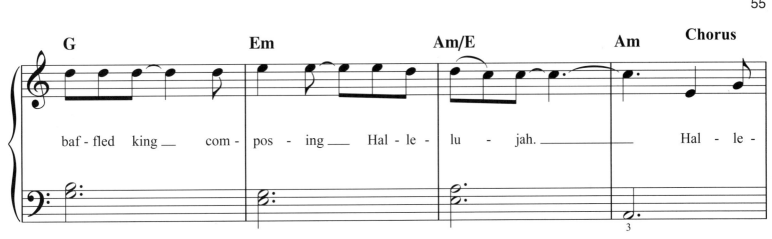

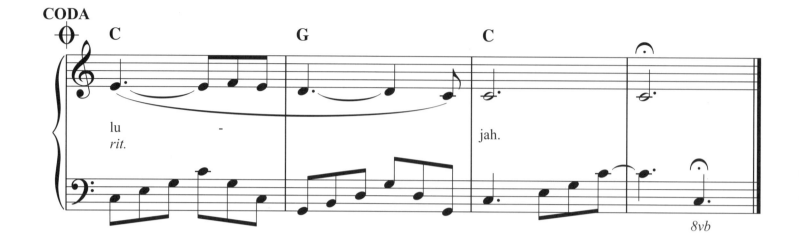

Additional Lyrics

2. Your faith was strong, but you needed proof.
   You saw her bathing on the roof.
   Her beauty and the moonlight overthrew you.
   She tied you to a kitchen chair.
   She broke your throne; she cut your hair.
   And from your lips she drew the Hallelujah.

3. Maybe I have been here before.
   I know this room; I've walked this floor.
   I used to live alone before I knew you.
   I've seen your flag on the marble arch.
   Love is not a victory march.
   It's a cold and it's a broken Hallelujah.

4. There was a time you let me know
   What's real and going on below.
   But now you never show it to me, do you?
   And remember when I moved in you,
   The holy dark was movin' too,
   And every breath we drew was Hallelujah.

5. Maybe there's a God above,
   And all I ever learned from love
   Was how to shoot at someone who outdrew you.
   And it's not a cry you can hear at night.
   It's not somebody who's seen the light.
   It's a cold and it's a broken Hallelujah.

TRUE COLORS

Words and Music by BILLY STEINBERG
and TOM KELLY

Em7 · D7sus · Gsus · G

dark - ness in - side you makes you feel so small. __ But I see your
call me up be - cause you know I'll be there. __ And I'll see your

C · G/B · D · C · G/B

true col - ors shin - ing through. __ I see your true col - ors and

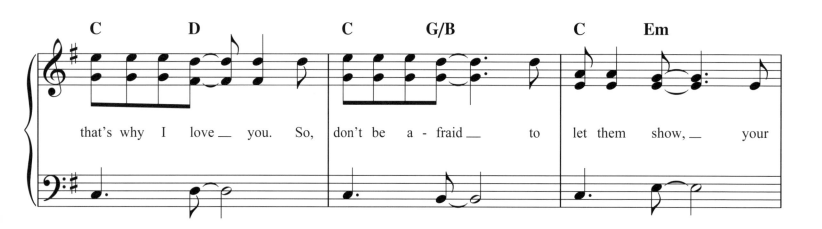

C · D · C · G/B · C · Em

that's why I love __ you. So, don't be a - fraid __ to let them show, __ your

To Coda

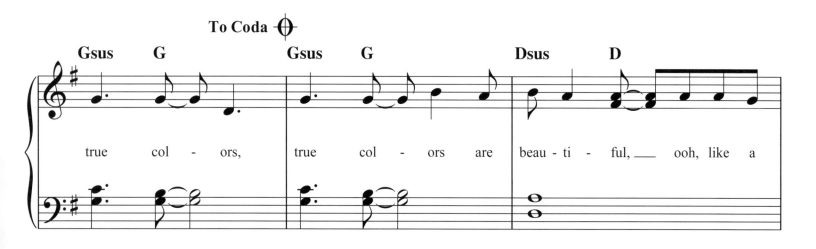

Gsus · G · Gsus · G · Dsus · D

true col - ors, true col - ors are beau - ti - ful, __ ooh, like a

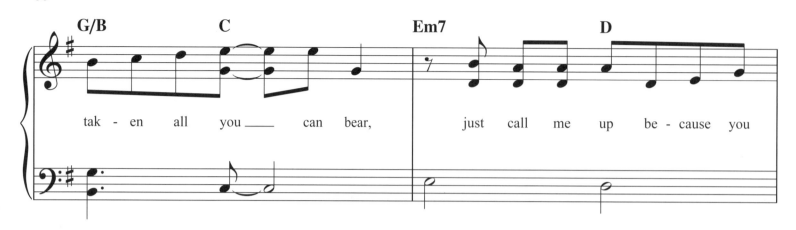

61

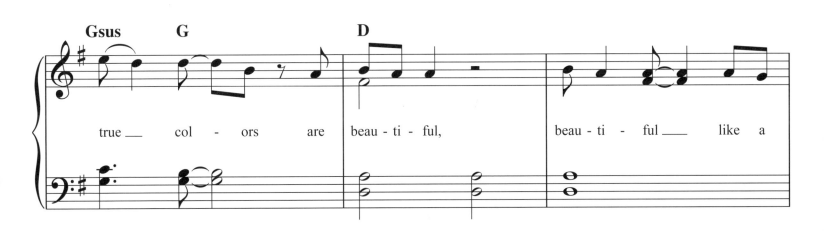

I BELIEVE I CAN FLY

from SPACE JAM

Words and Music by
ROBERT KELLY

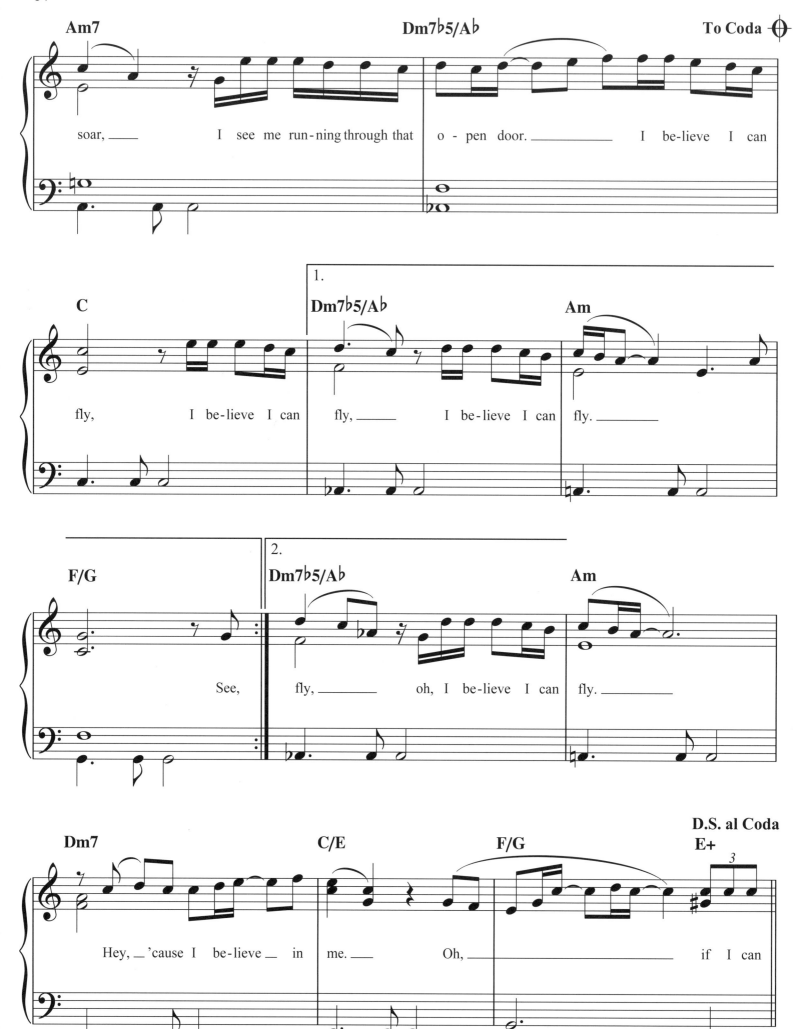

CODA

fly,   I be-lieve I can fly, _____ I be-lieve I can fly, _____ hey, if I just

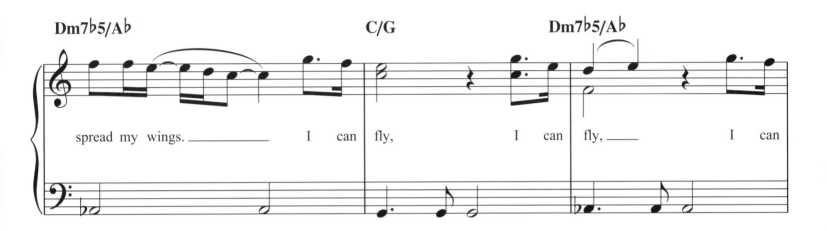

spread my wings. _____ I can fly,   I can fly, _____ I can

fly,   hey, if I just spread my wings. _____ I can fly.

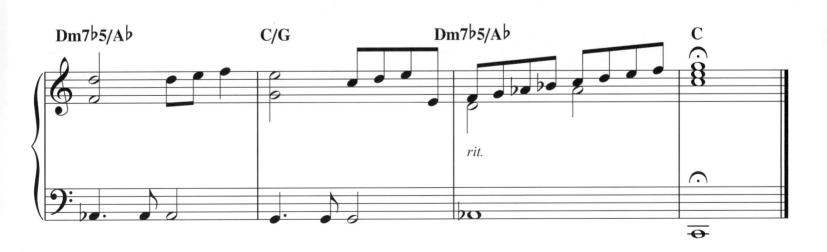

rit.

IMAGINE

Words and Music by
JOHN LENNON

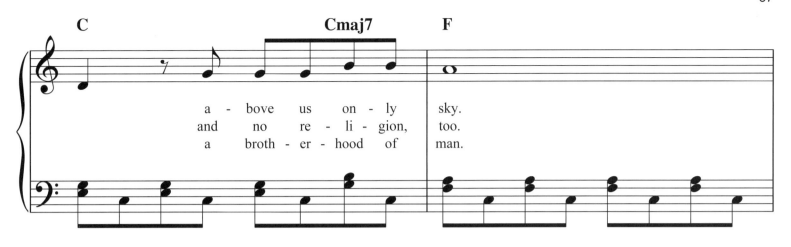

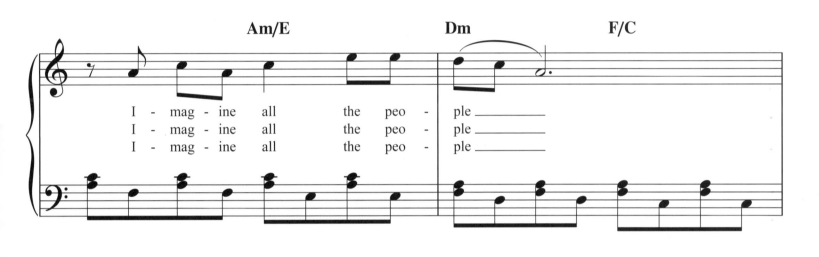

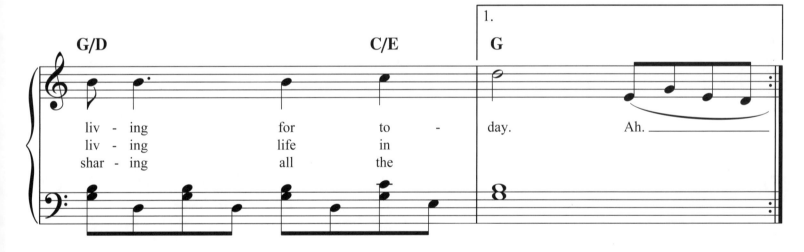

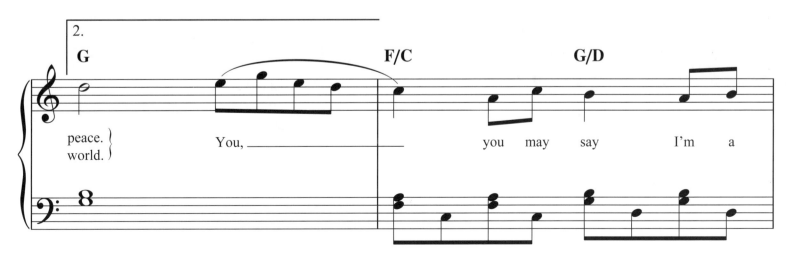

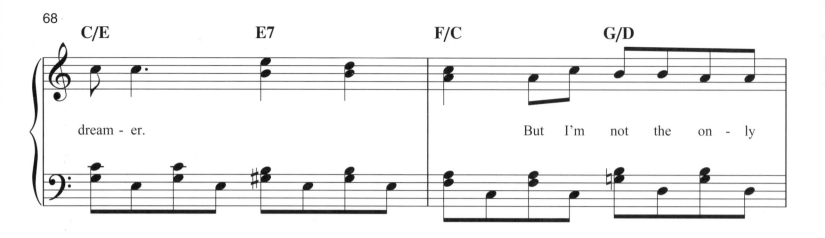

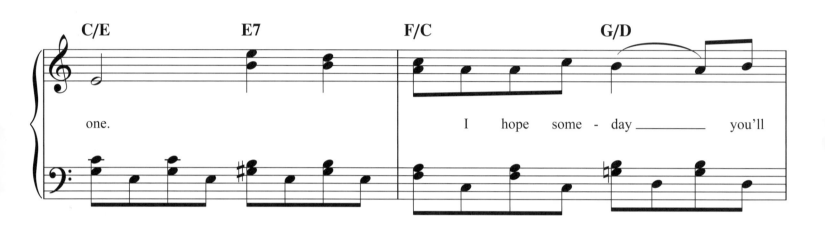

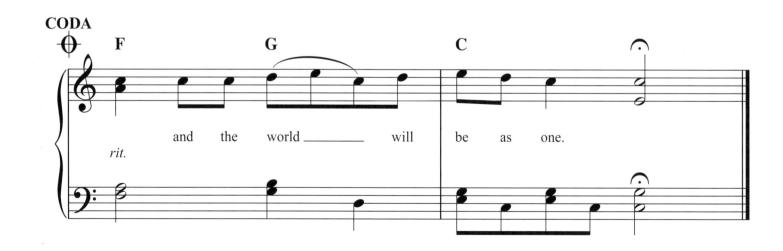

WE ARE THE CHAMPIONS

Words and Music by
FREDDIE MERCURY

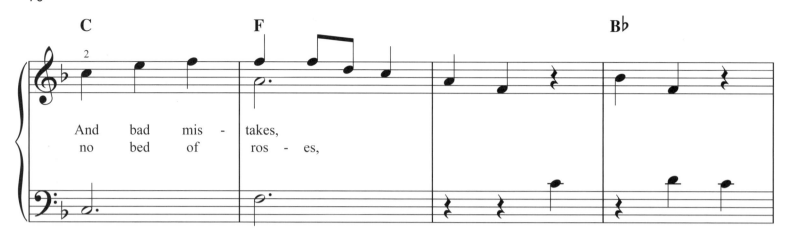

And bad mis - takes,
no bed of ros - es,

I've made a few. _____ cruise. _____
no pleas - ure I con -

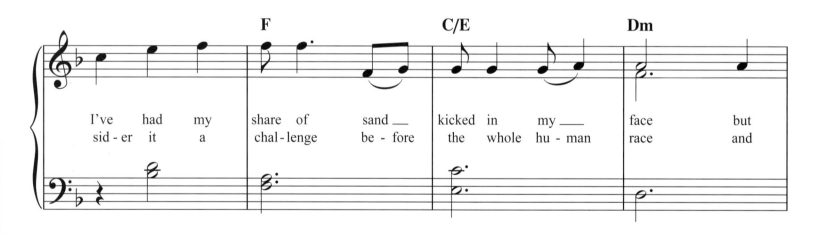

I've had my share of sand _ kicked in my ___ face but
sid - er it a chal - lenge be - fore the whole hu - man race and

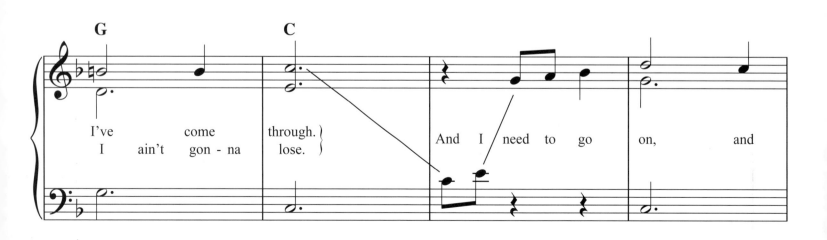

I've come through.
I ain't gon - na lose.
And I need to go on, and

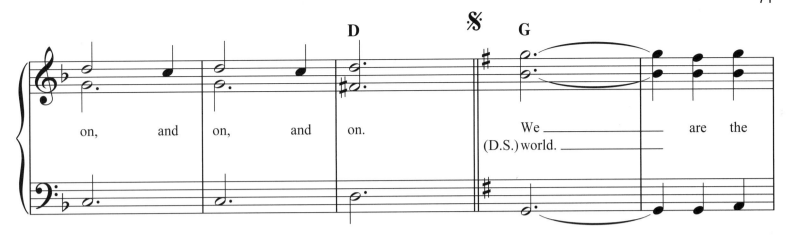

on, and on, and on. We _____ are the
(D.S.) world. _____

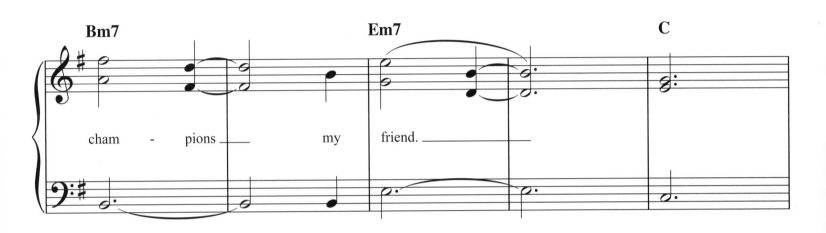

cham - pions _____ my friend. _____

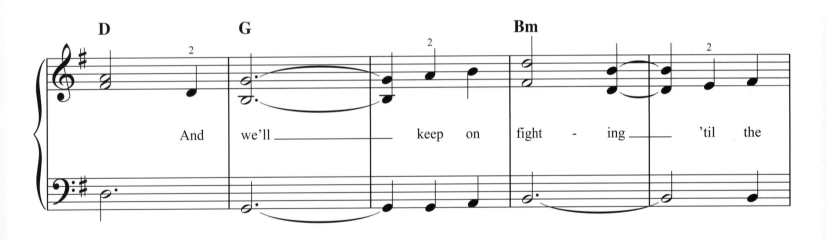

And we'll _____ keep on fight - ing _____ 'til the

end. _____ We

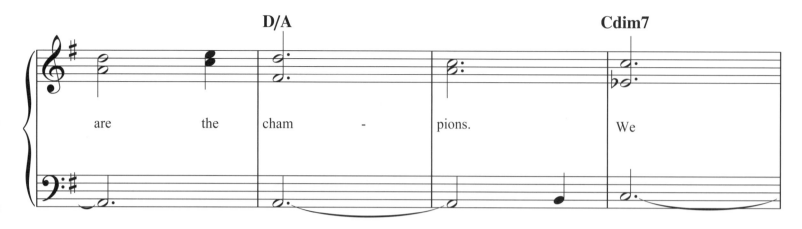

are the cham - pions. We

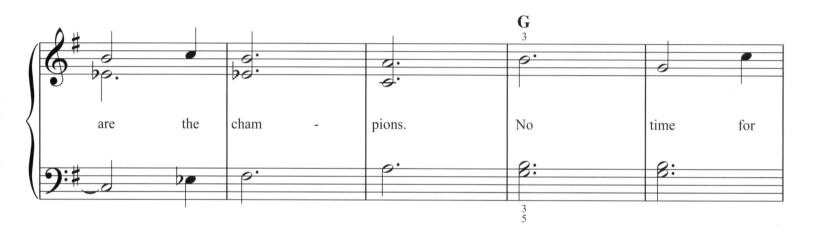

are the cham - pions. No time for

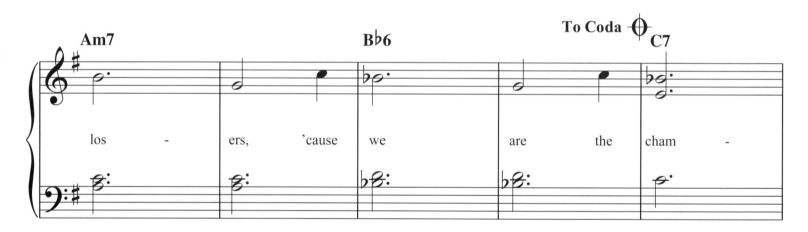

los - ers, 'cause we are the cham -

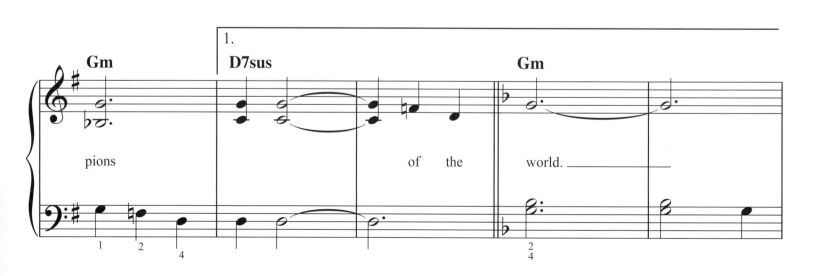

pions of the world.

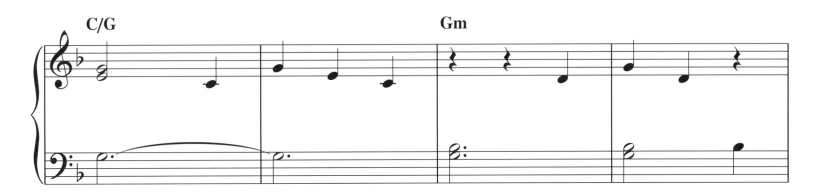

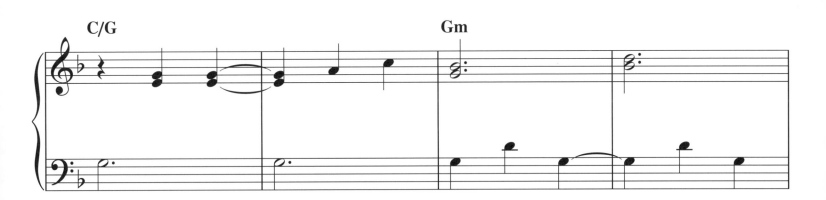

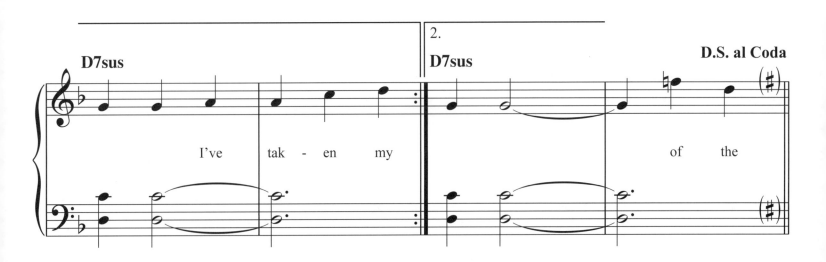

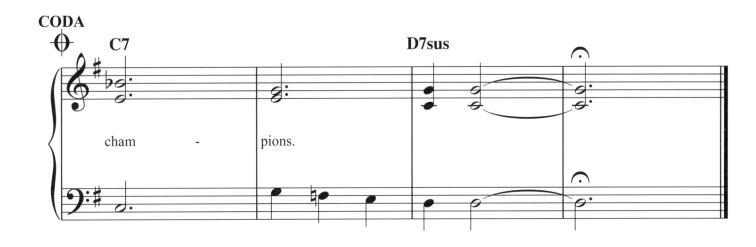

IT'S MY LIFE

Words and Music by JON BON JOVI,
MARTIN SANDBERG and RICHIE SAMBORA

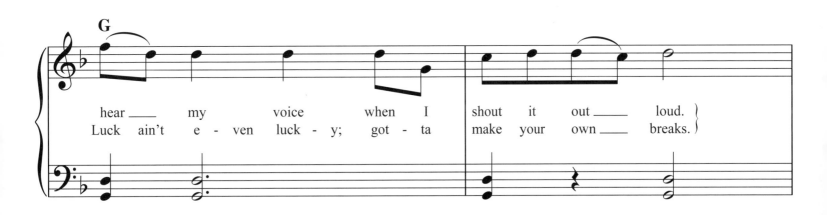

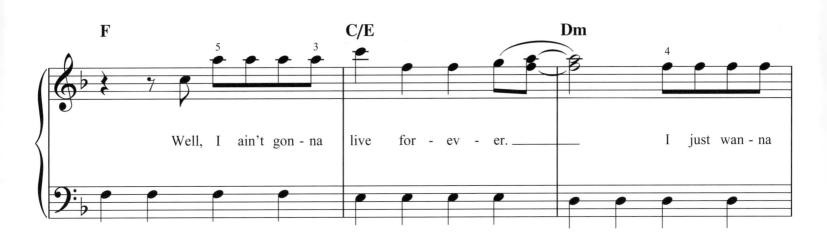

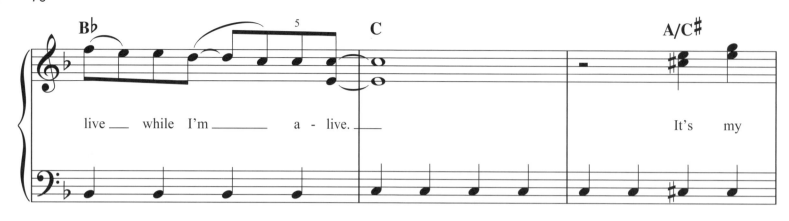

live ___ while I'm _____ a - live. ___ It's my

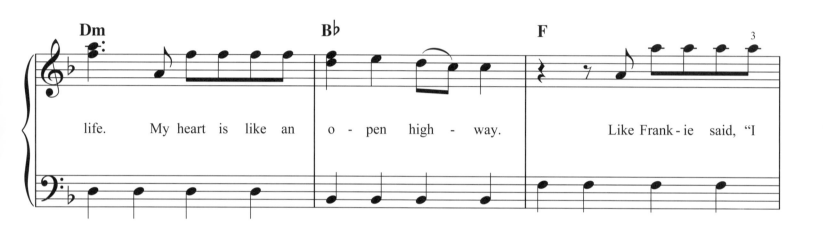

life. My heart is like an o - pen high - way. Like Frank - ie said, "I

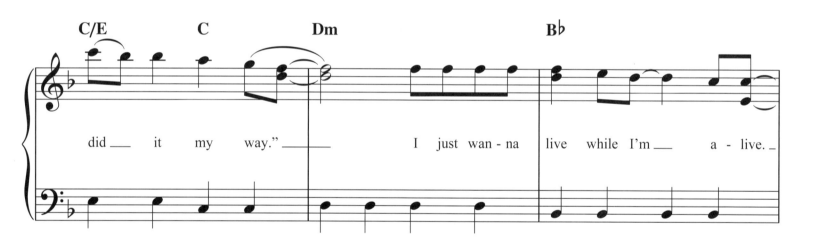

did ___ it my way." ___ I just wan - na live while I'm ___ a - live. ___

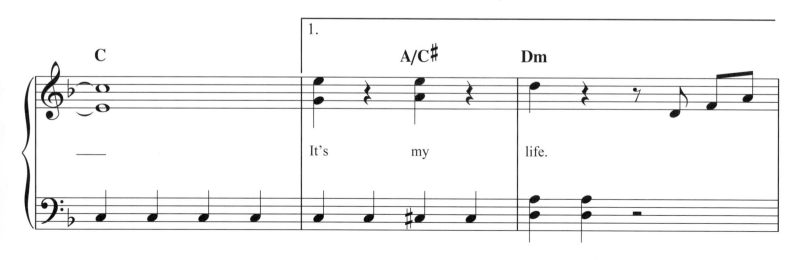

It's my life.

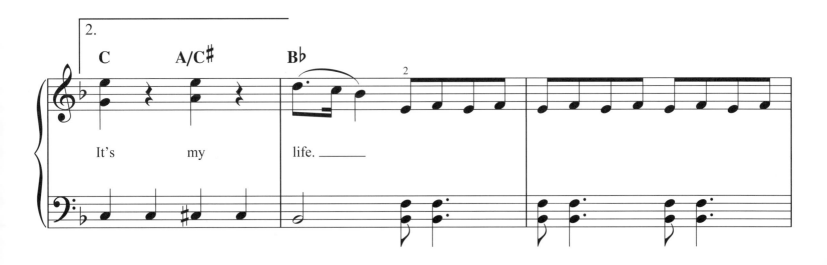

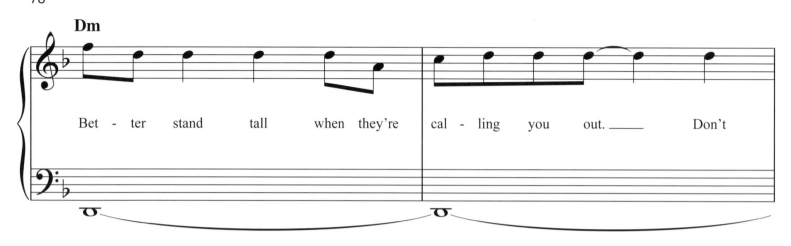

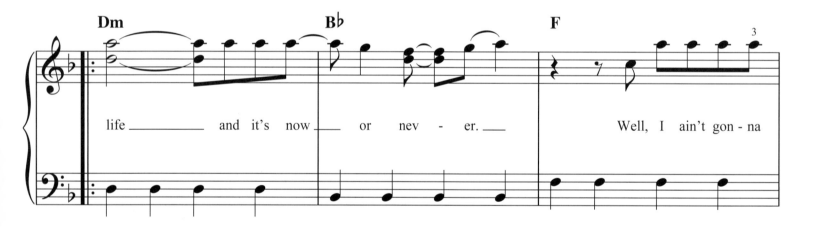

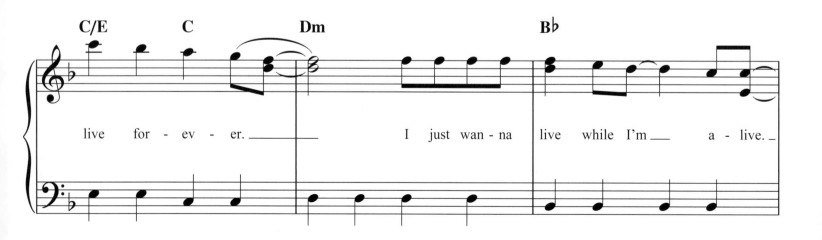

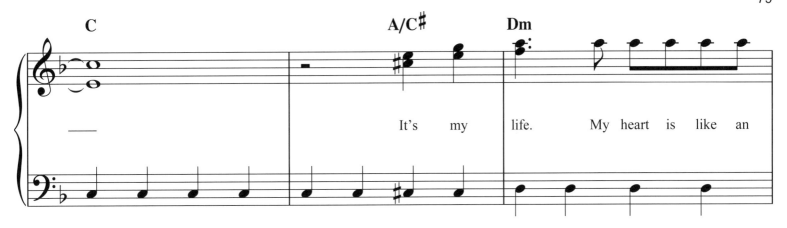

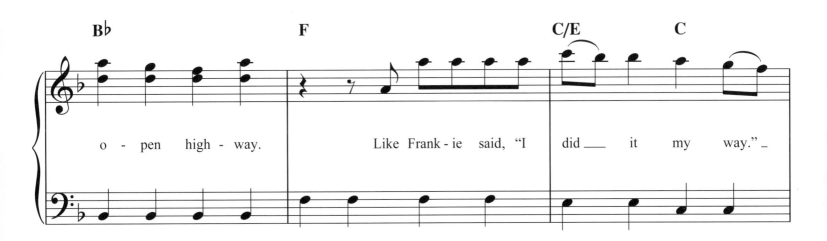

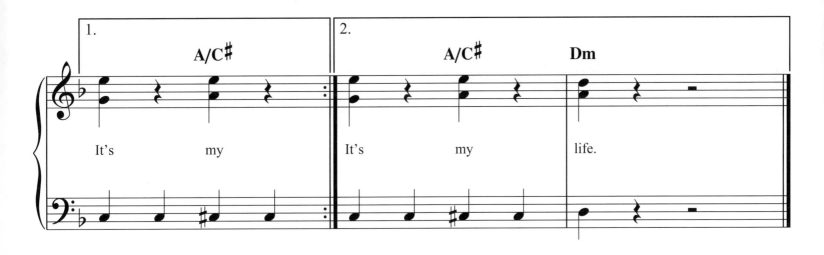

ONE MOMENT IN TIME

Words and Music by ALBERT HAMMOND
and JOHN BETTIS

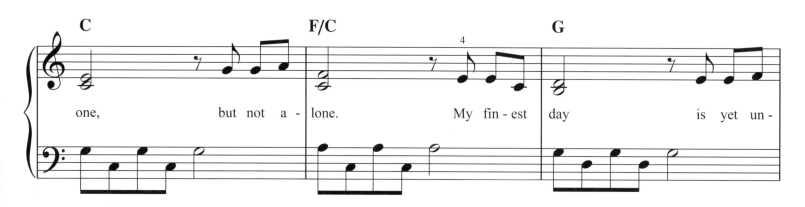

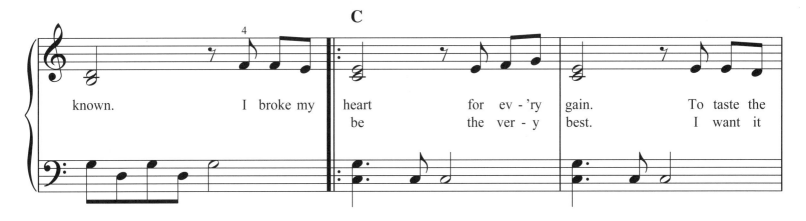

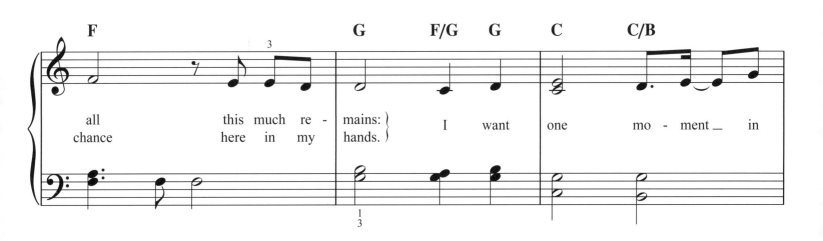

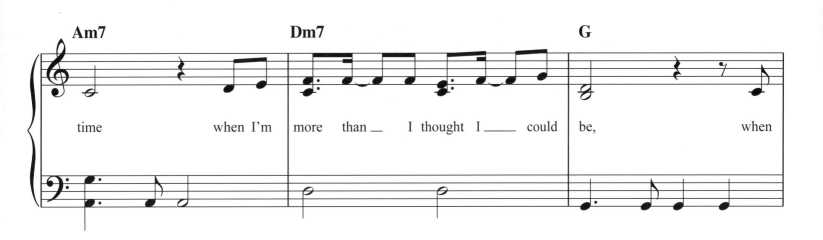

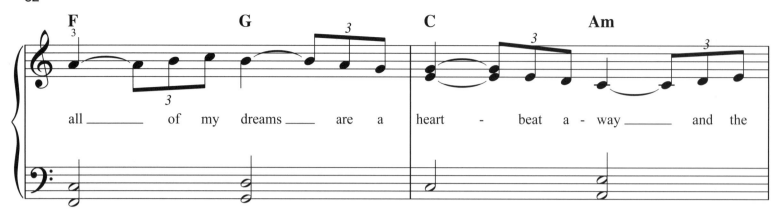

all _____ of my dreams _____ are a heart - beat a - way _____ and the

an - swers _ are all up _ to me.   Give me _____ one mo - ment _ in

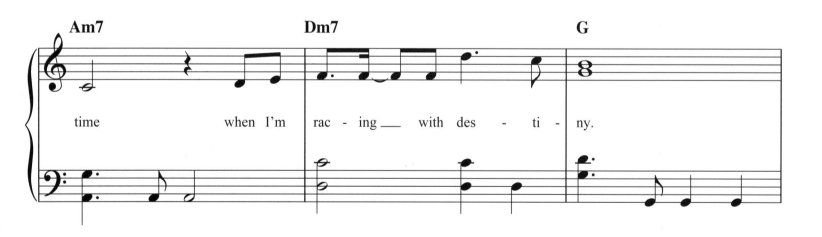

time   when I'm rac - ing _ with des - ti - ny.

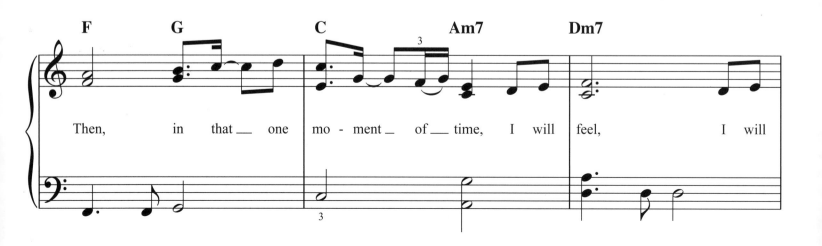

Then,   in that _ one mo - ment _ of _ time, I will feel,   I will

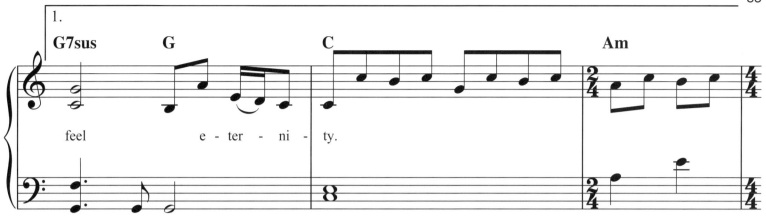

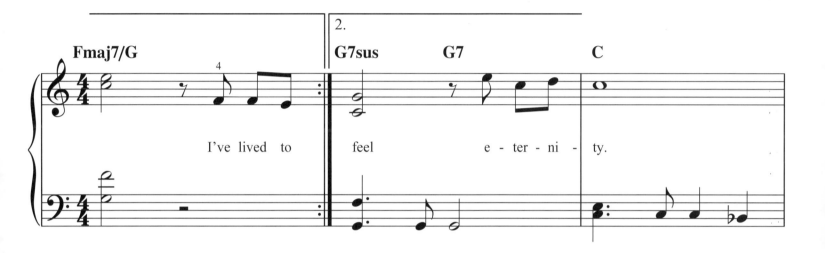

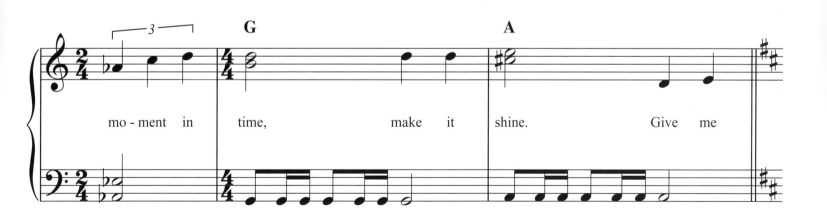

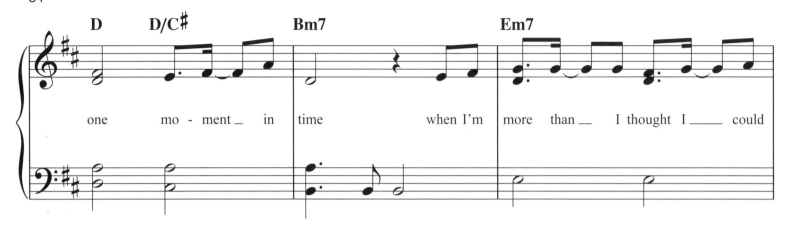

one mo - ment_ in time   when I'm   more than _ I thought I _____ could

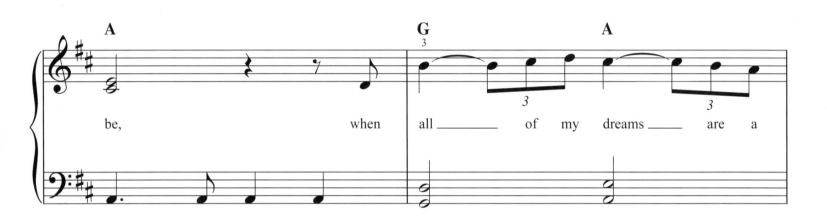

be,   when   all _____ of my dreams _____ are a

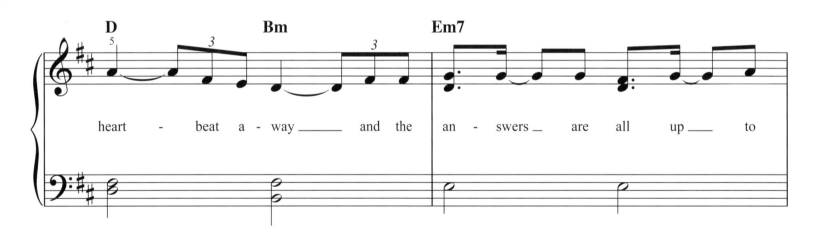

heart - beat a - way _____ and the   an - swers _ are all   up _ to

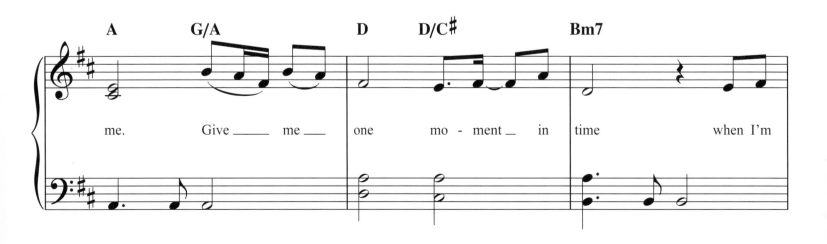

me.   Give _____ me _____   one   mo - ment _ in   time   when I'm

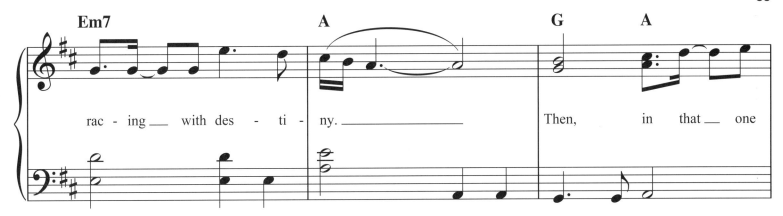

rac - ing ___ with des - ti - ny. _____ Then, in that ___ one

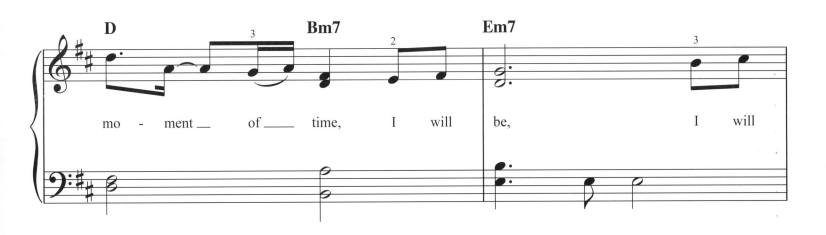

mo - ment ___ of ___ time, I will be, I will

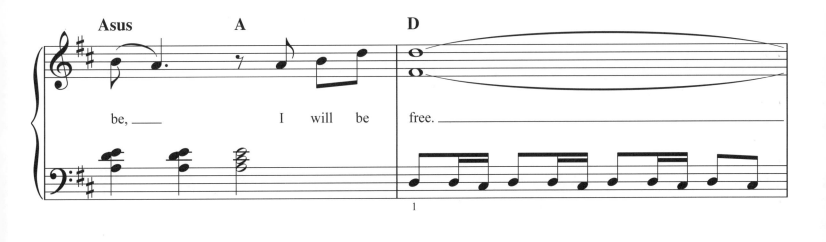

be, ___ I will be free. _____

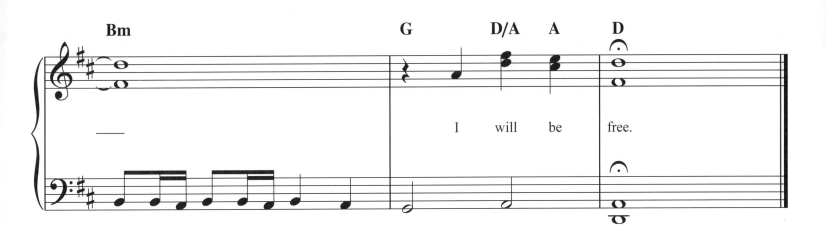

I will be free.

REACH

Words and Music by GLORIA ESTEFAN
and DIANE WARREN

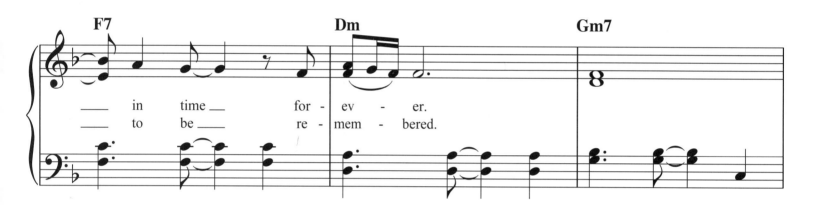

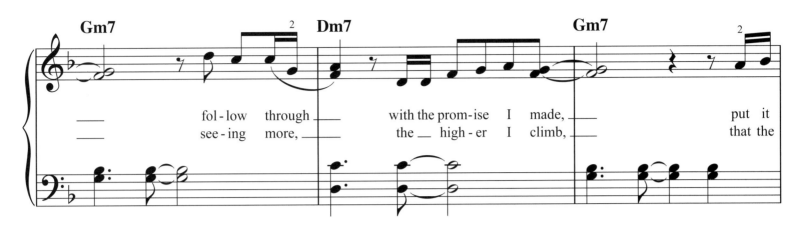

88

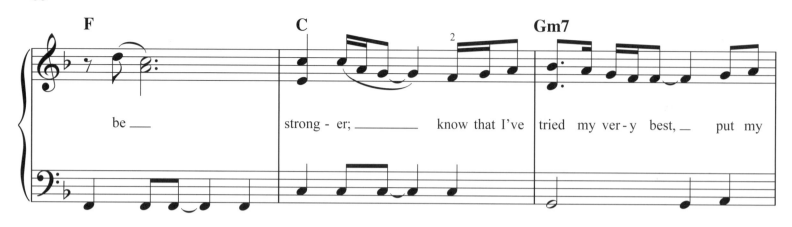

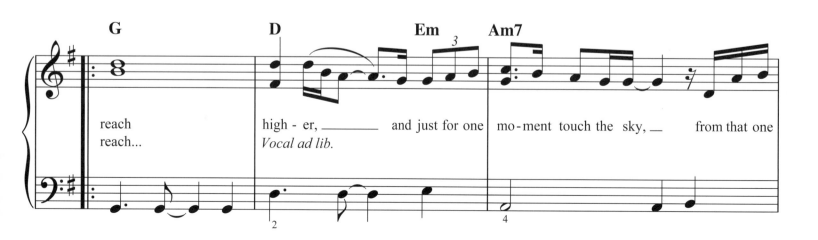

mo-ment in ____ my life, I'm gon-na be, _____ I'm gon-na be so much

strong - er, yes, ___ I am; I put my spir - it to the test. ___ If I could

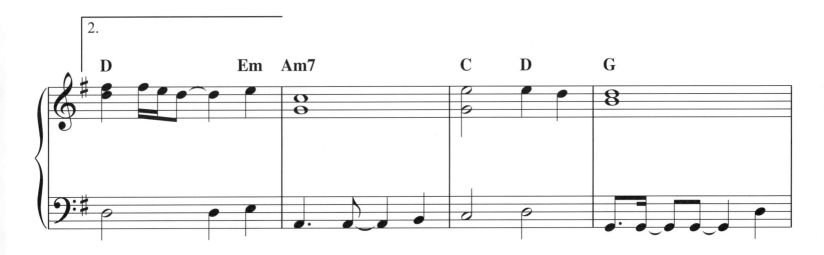

RETURN TO INNOCENCE

Words and Music by
CURLY M.C.

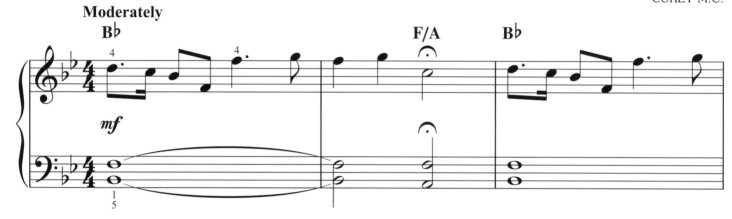

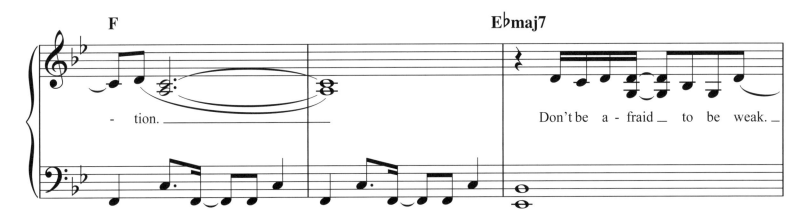

The re - turn to in - no - cence.

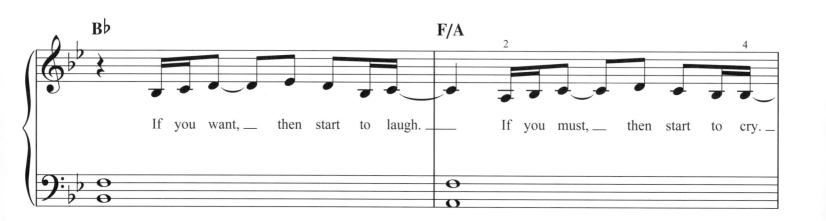

If you want, __ then start to laugh. __ If you must, __ then start to cry. __

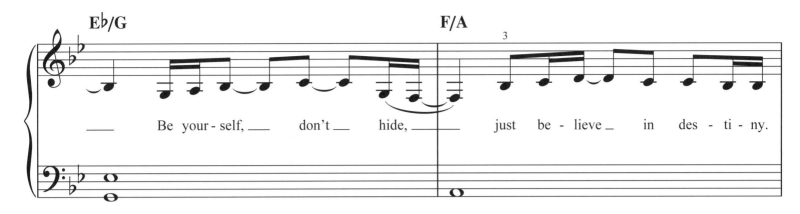

Be your-self, ___ don't ___ hide, ___ just be - lieve ___ in des - ti - ny.

Don't care _____ what peo - ple say, just fol - low your own ___

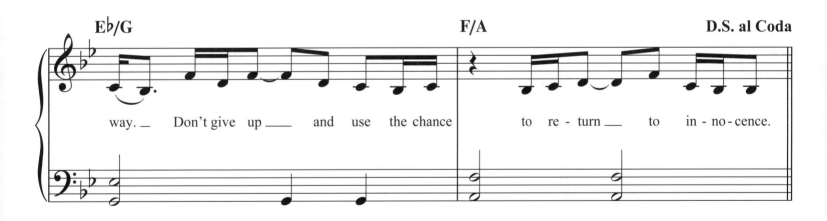

way. ___ Don't give up ___ and use the chance to re - turn ___ to in - no - cence.

94

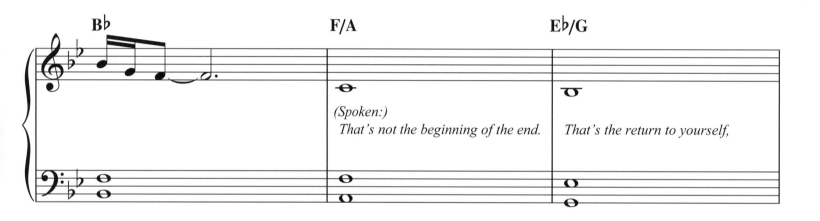

(Spoken:)
That's not the beginning of the end.   *That's the return to yourself,*

the return to innocence.

(Spoken:)
That's the return to innocence.

STRONGER
(What Doesn't Kill You)

Words and Music by GREG KURSTIN,
ALEXANDRA TAMPOSI, DAVID GAMSON
and JORGEN ELOFSSON

Moderately

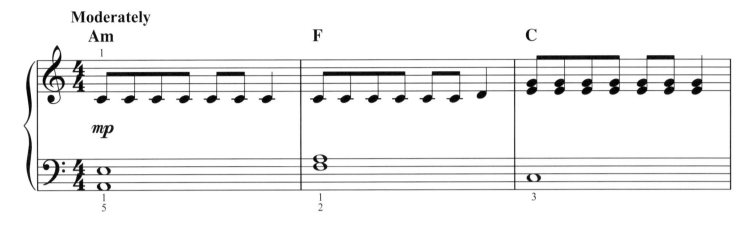

You know the bed feels warm - er _____

sleep - in' here a - lone. You know I dream in

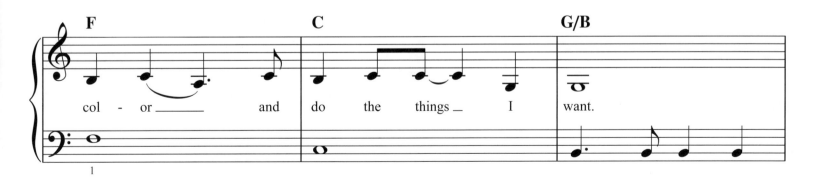

col - or _____ and do the things _____ I want.

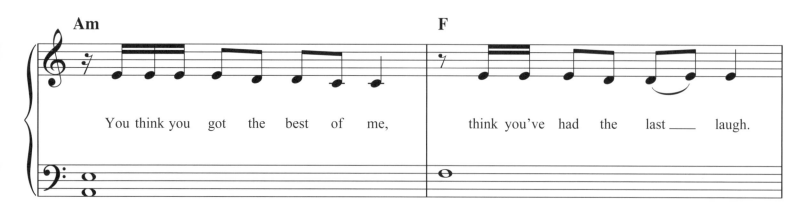

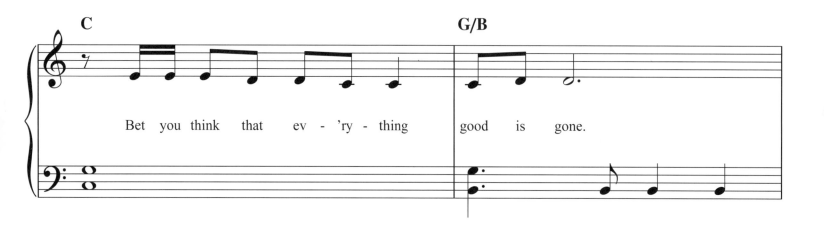

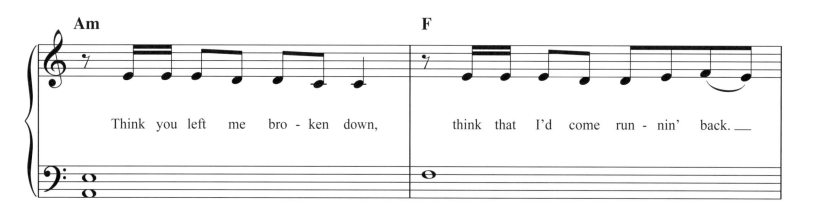

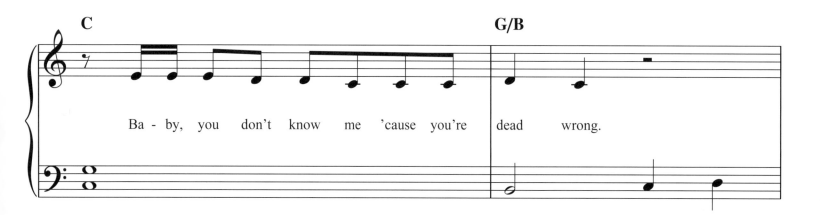

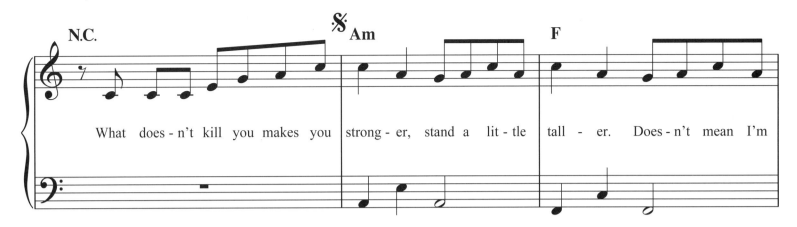

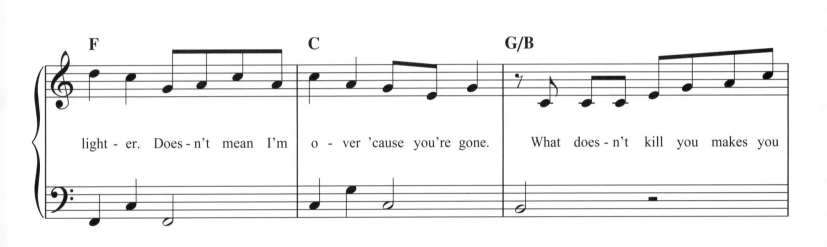

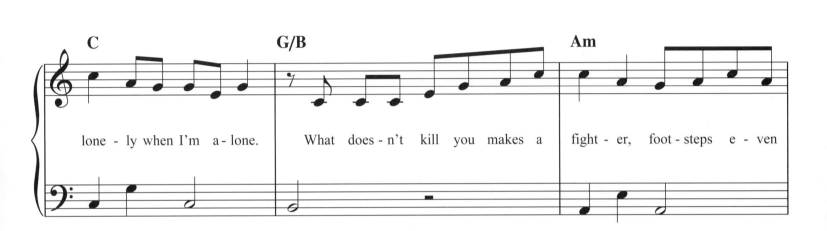

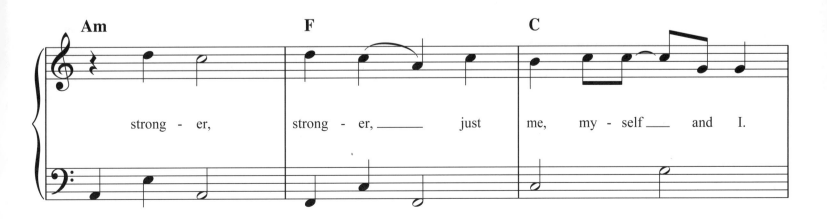

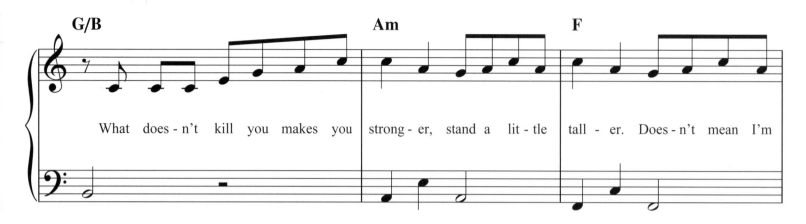

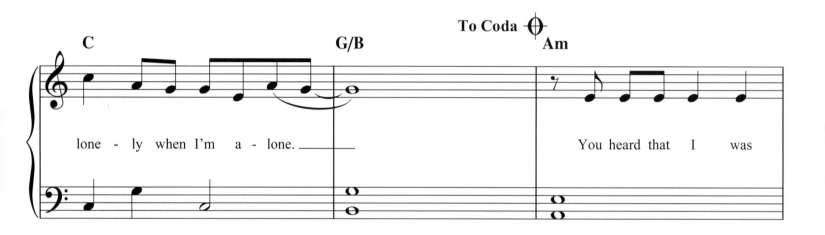

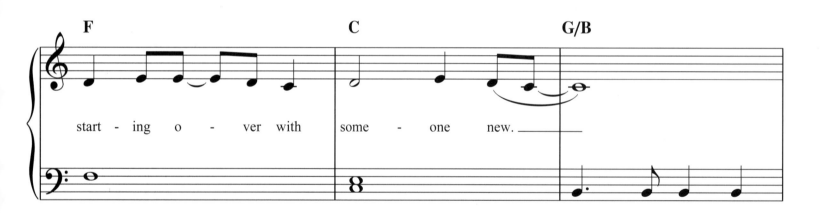

You did-n't think that I'd come back, I'd come back swing - in'.

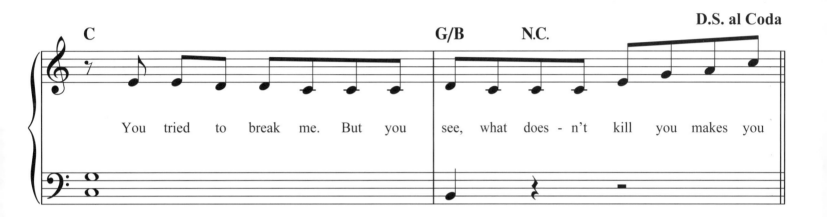

You tried to break me. But you see, what does-n't kill you makes you

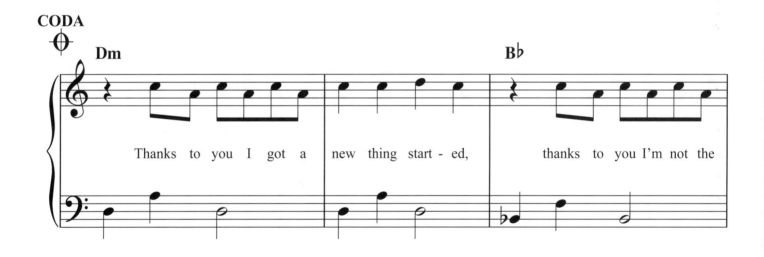

Thanks to you I got a new thing start - ed, thanks to you I'm not the

bro - ken - heart - ed. Thanks to you I'm fi - n'ly think - in' 'bout me. You

know in the end, __ the day I left was just - a my be - gin - ning. ____

In the __ end, _____ what does - n't kill you makes you strong - er, stand a lit - tle

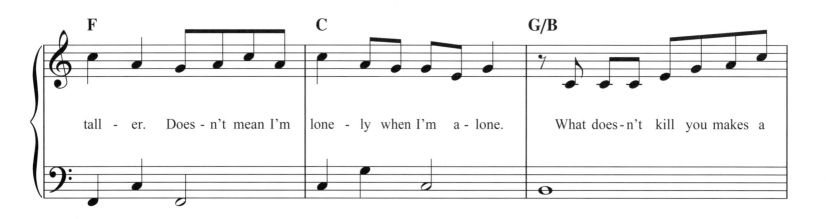

tall - er. Does - n't mean I'm lone - ly when I'm a - lone. What does - n't kill you makes a

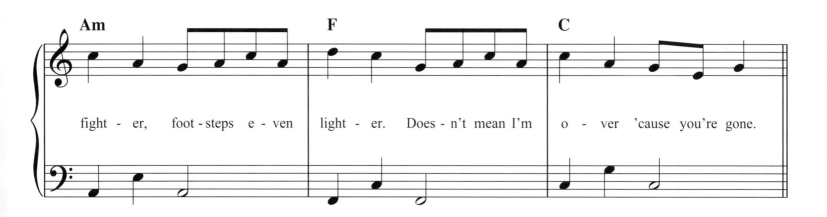

fight - er, foot - steps e - ven light - er. Does - n't mean I'm o - ver 'cause you're gone.

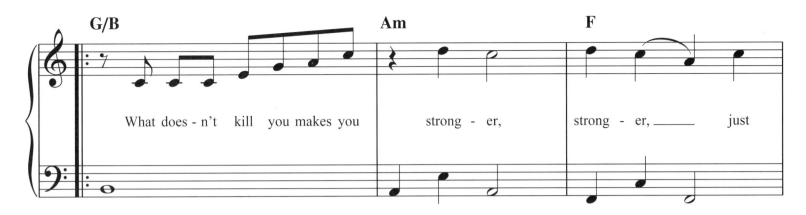

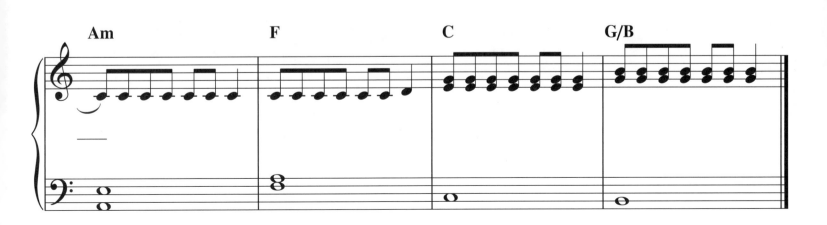

WALKING ON SUNSHINE

Words and Music by
KIMBERLEY REW

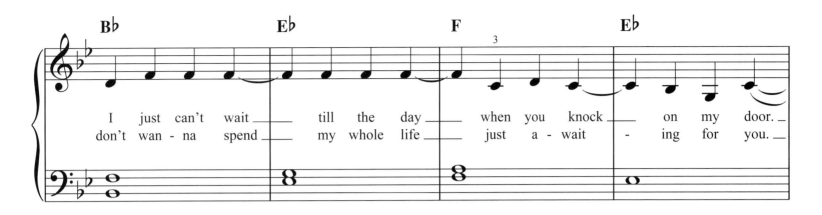

I just can't wait _____ till the day _____ when you knock _____ on my door. _____
don't wan - na spend _____ my whole life _____ just a - wait _____ - ing for you. _____

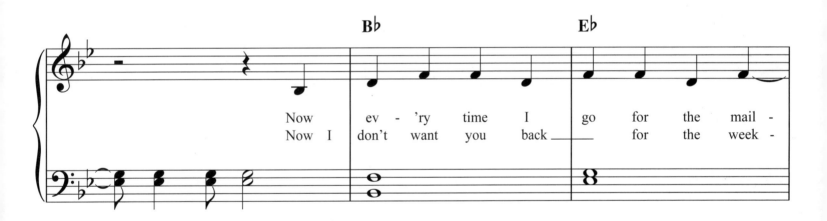

Now ev - 'ry time I go for the mail -
Now I don't want you back _____ for the week -

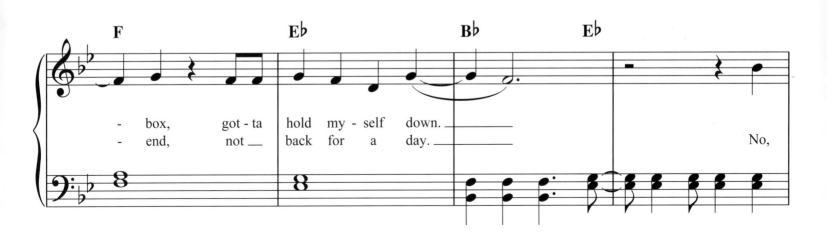

- box, got - ta hold my - self down. _____
- end, not _____ back for a day. _____ No,

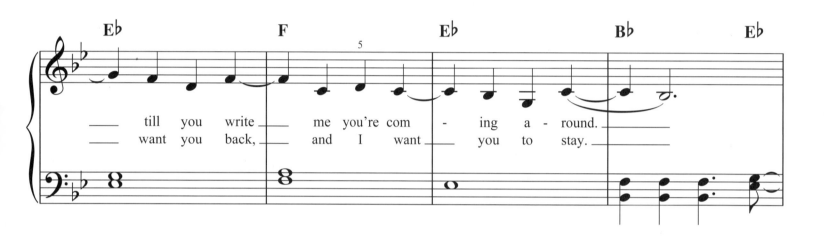

Whoa. _____ I'm walk-ing on ___ sun - shine.

Whoa, _____ and don't it feel ___ good!

All right now, and don't it feel ___ good!

Hey! I

106

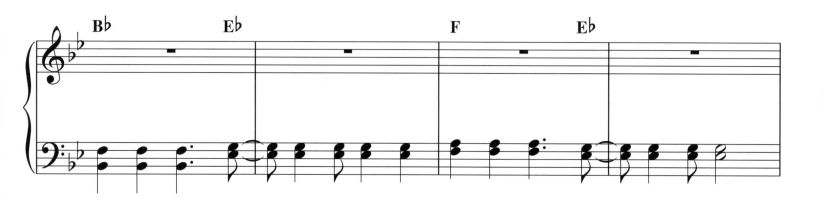

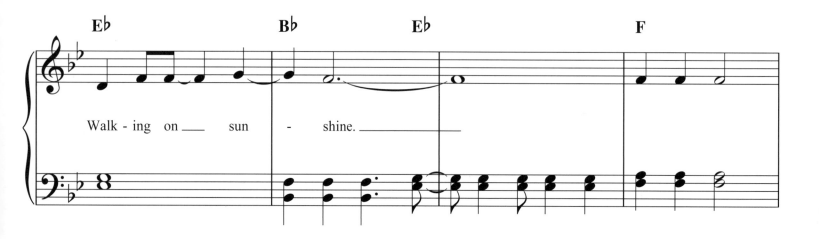

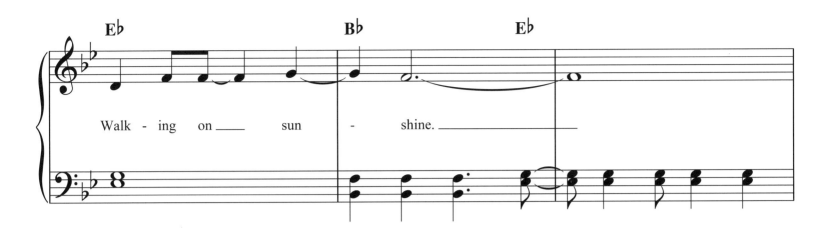

I'm on ___ sun - shine, ba - by. Oh, oh,

yeah. I'm on ___ sun - shine, ba - by. Oh, ___ I'm

D.S. al Coda

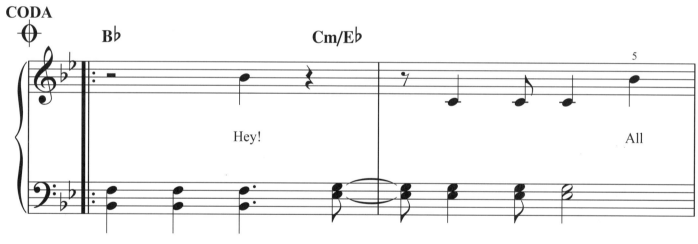

CODA

Hey! All

right now, and don't it feel ___ good! don't it feel ___ good!

YOU RAISE ME UP

Words and Music by BRENDAN GRAHAM
and ROLF LØVLAND

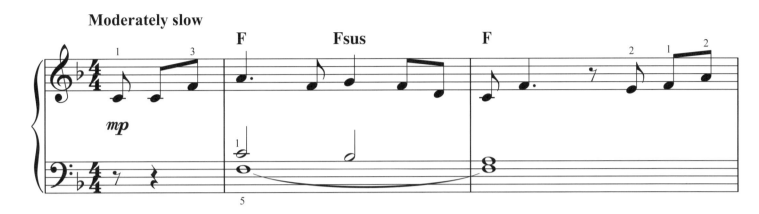

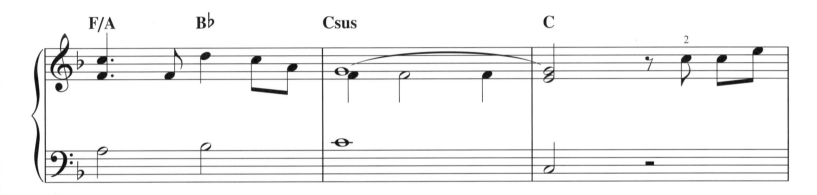

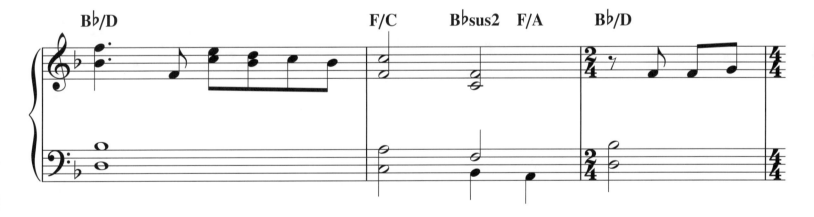

When I am down and, oh, my soul so wea - ry, when trou - bles

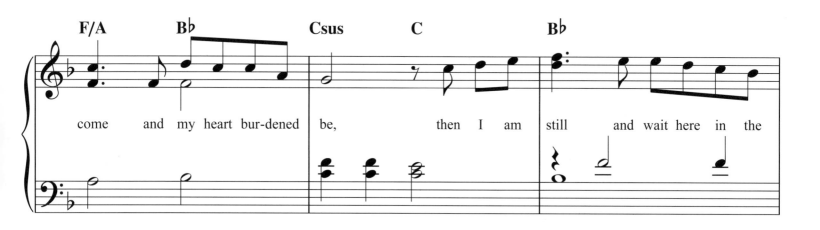

come and my heart bur-dened be, then I am still and wait here in the

si - lence un - til you come and sit a while with

me. You raise me up so I can stand on moun - tains. You raise me

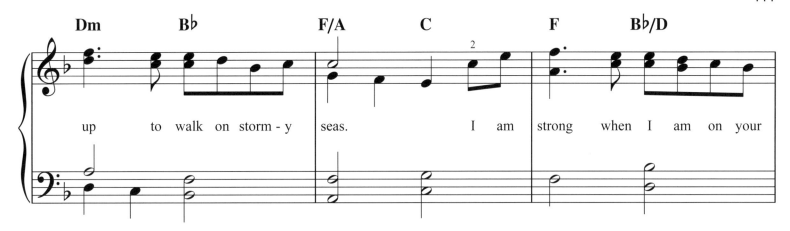

up   to walk on storm-y   seas.   I   am   strong   when I   am   on   your

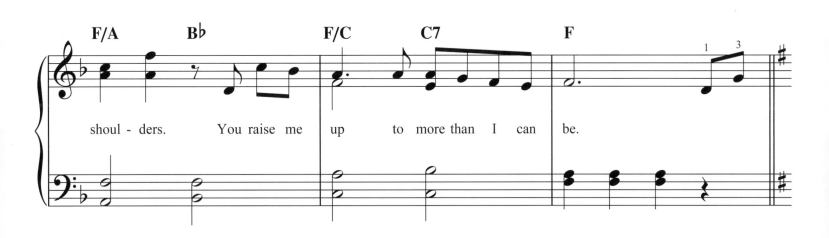

shoul - ders.   You raise me   up   to more than   I   can   be.

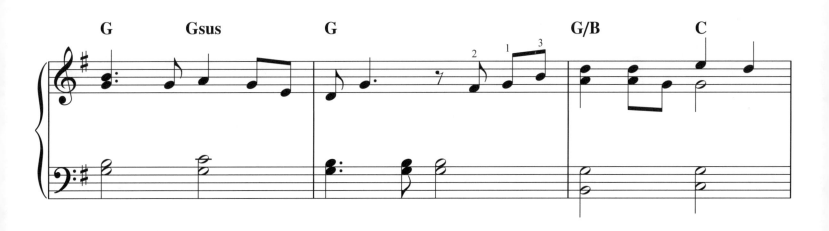

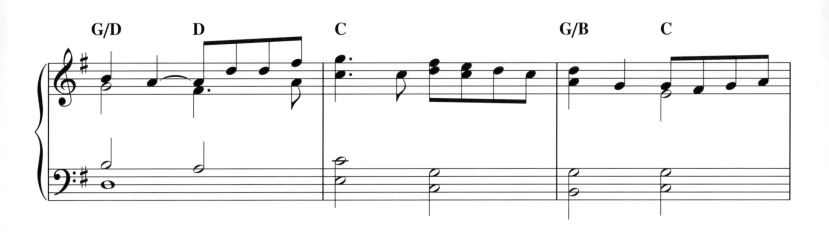

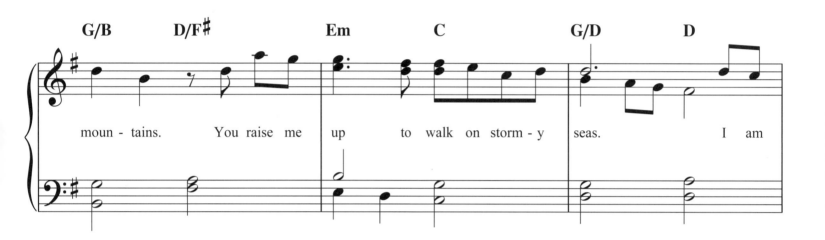

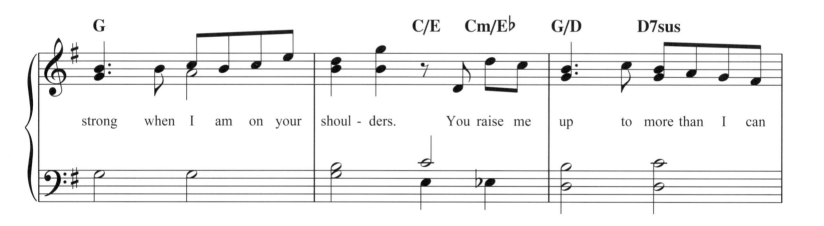

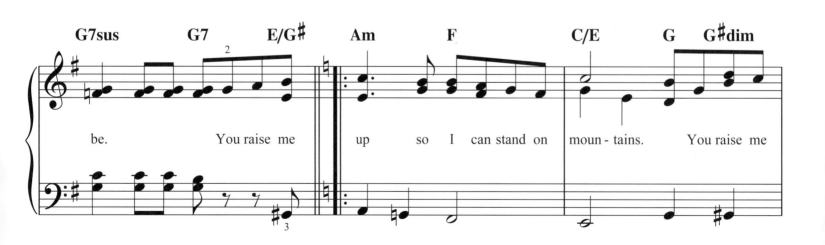

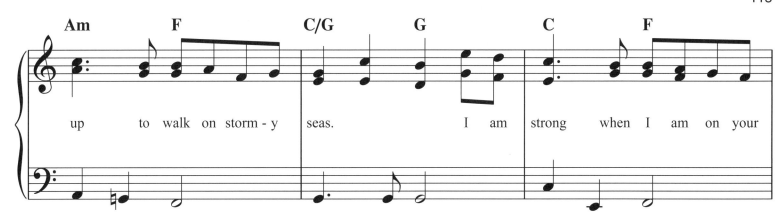

up   to walk on storm-y   seas.   I am   strong   when I am on your

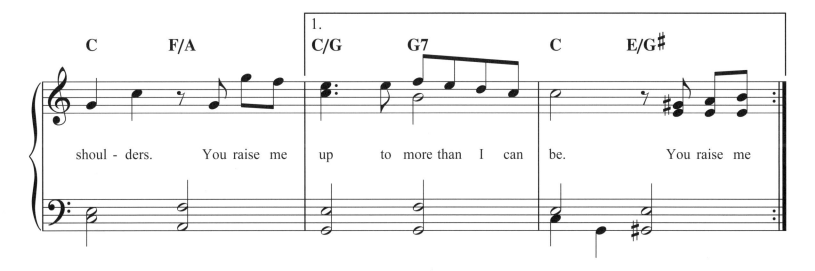

shoul-ders.   You raise me   up   to more than I can   be.   You raise me

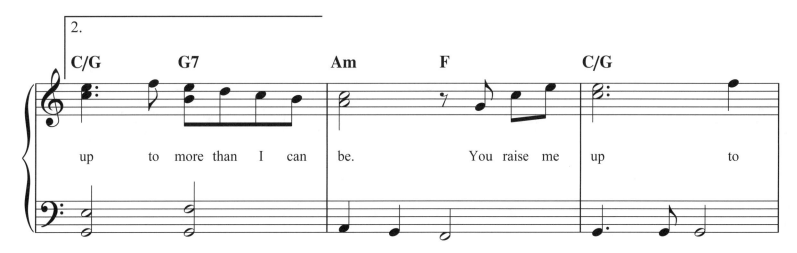

up   to more than I can   be.   You raise me   up   to

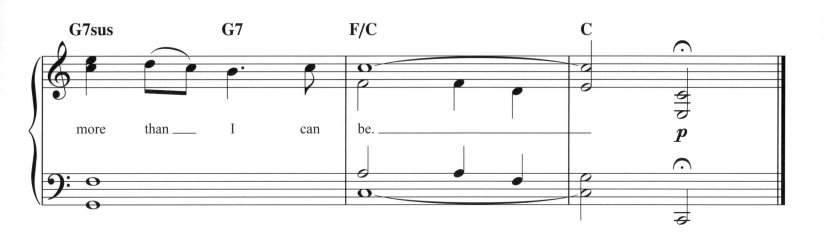

more   than ___ I   can   be. ___

WHEN YOU BELIEVE

from THE PRINCE OF EGYPT

Words and Music by
STEPHEN SCHWARTZ

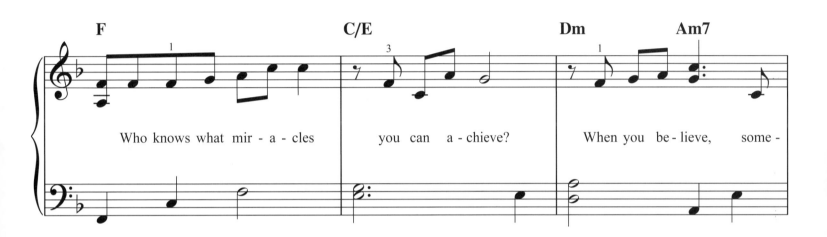

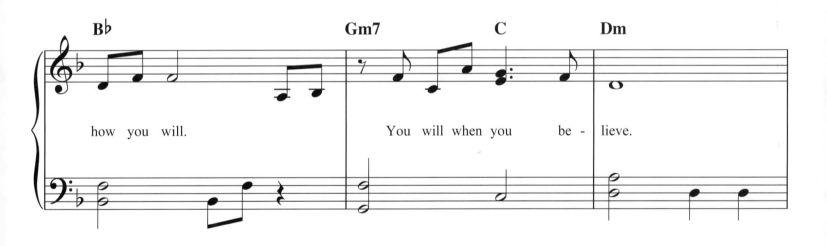

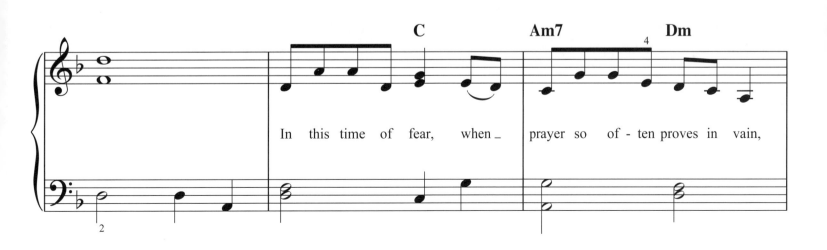

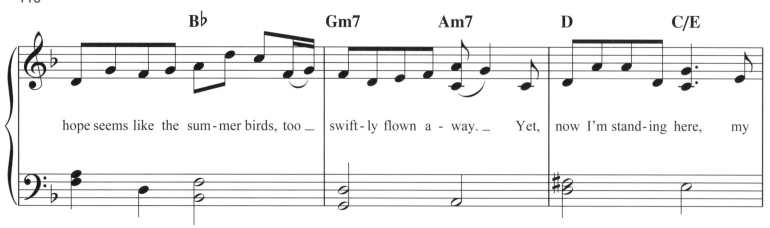

hope seems like the sum-mer birds, too _ swift-ly flown a - way. _ Yet, now I'm stand-ing here, my

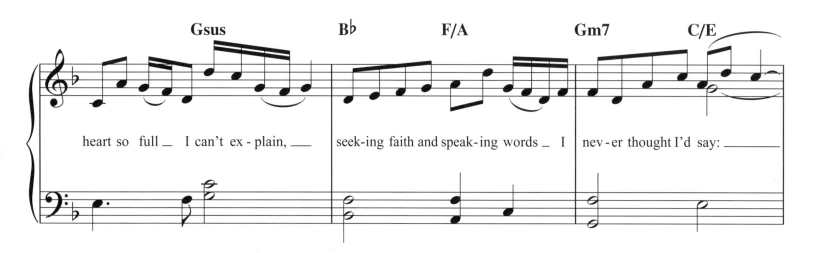

heart so full _ I can't ex - plain, ___ seek-ing faith and speak-ing words _ I nev - er thought I'd say: _____

___ There can be mir - a - cles when you be - lieve.

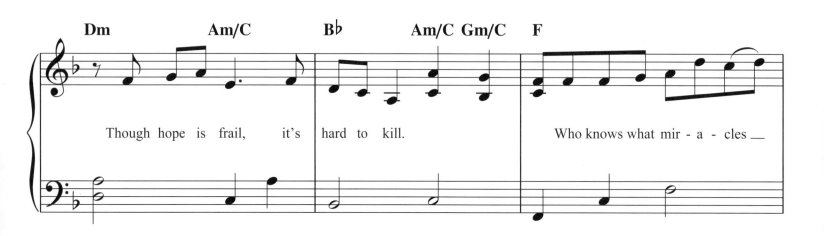

Though hope is frail, it's hard to kill. Who knows what mir - a - cles ___

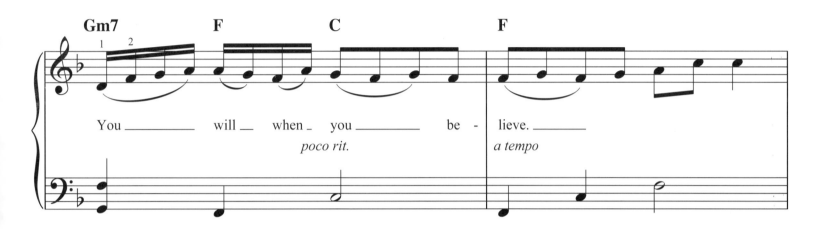

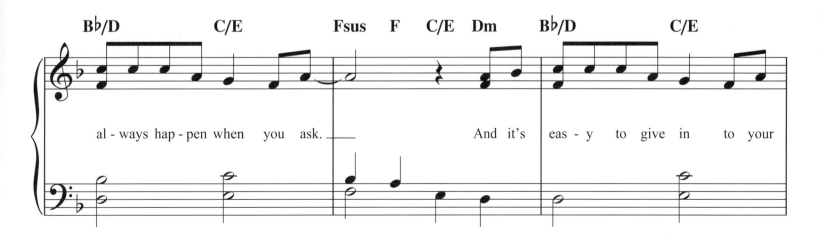

fear.   But   when you're blind-ed by your pain, can't   see your way clear through the rain,   a

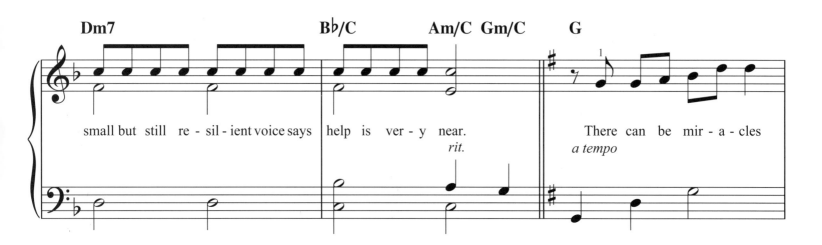

small but still re - sil - ient voice says help is ver - y near.   There can be mir - a - cles

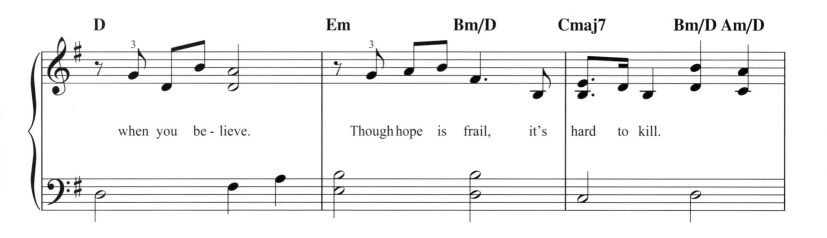

when you be - lieve.   Though hope is frail, it's hard to kill.

Who knows what mir - a - cles   you can a - chieve?   When you be - lieve,   some-

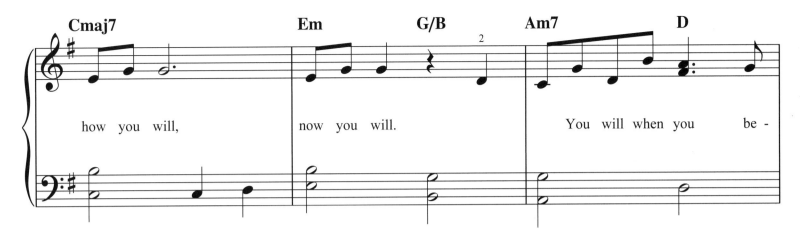

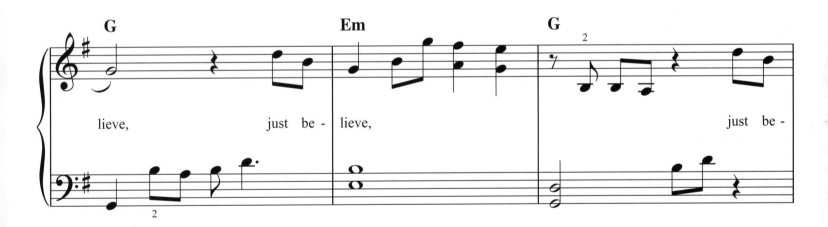

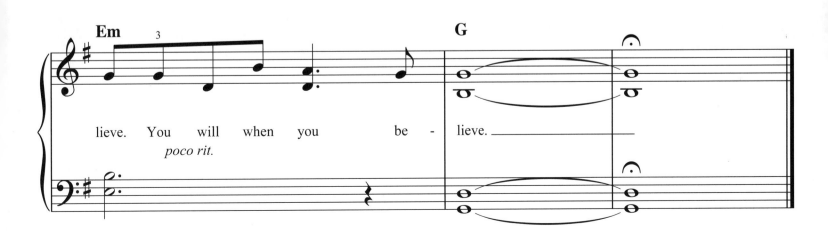

THE WIND BENEATH MY WINGS

from the Original Motion Picture BEACHES

Words and Music by LARRY HENLEY
and JEFF SILBAR

You've been con - tent ___ to let me shine, ___
on - ly a face ___ with - out a name, ___
I want you to know ___ I know the truth; ___

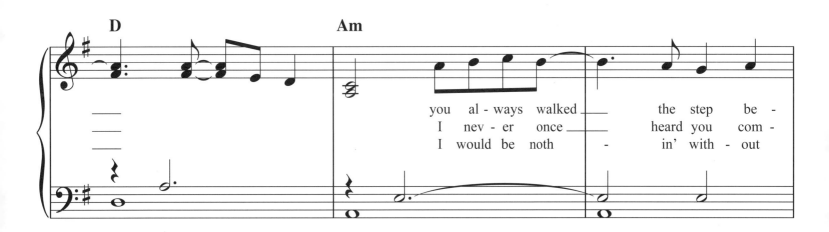

you al - ways walked ___ the step be -
I nev - er once ___ heard you com -
I would be noth - in' with - out

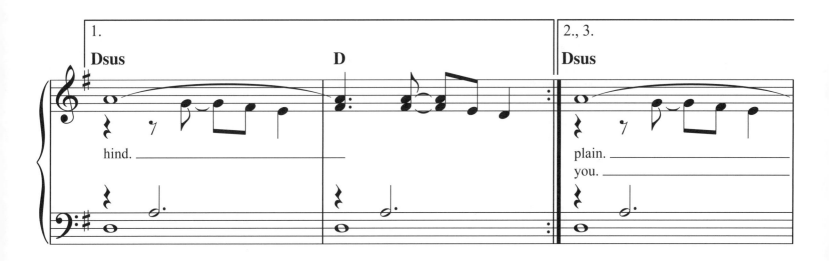

hind. ___
plain. ___
you. ___

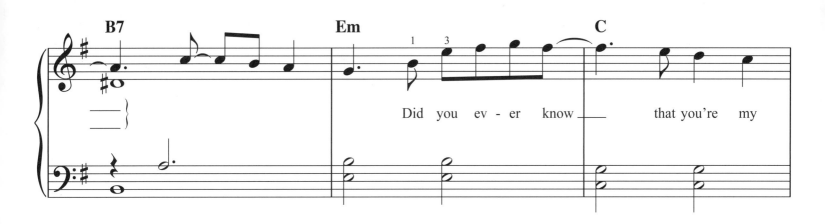

Did you ev - er know ___ that you're my

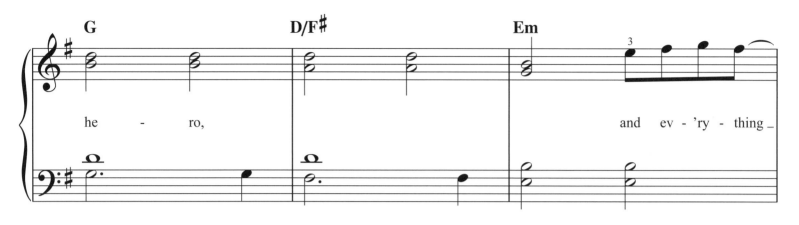

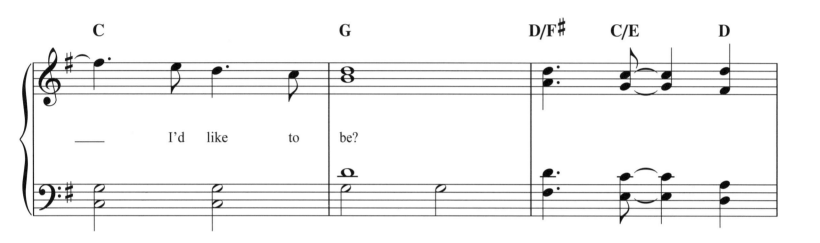

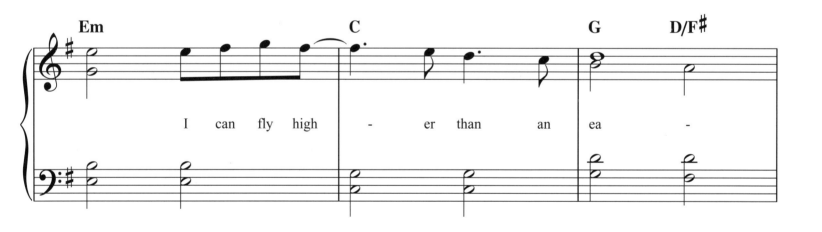

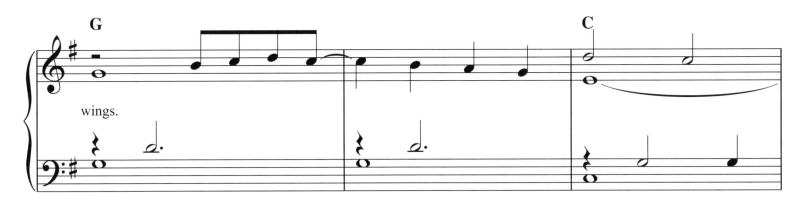

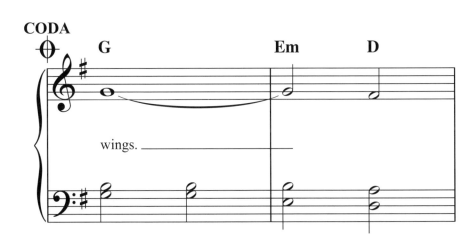

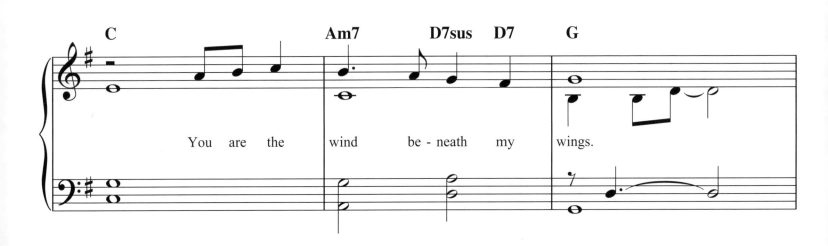

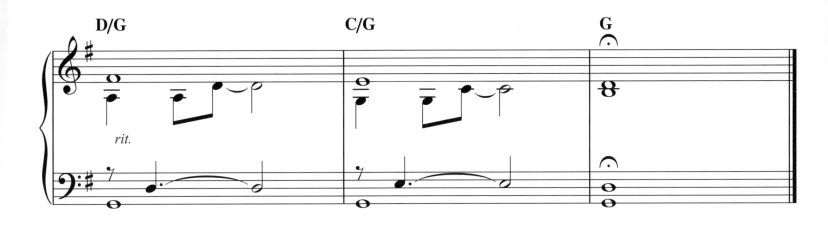

YOU'RE THE INSPIRATION

Words and Music by PETER CETERA
and DAVID FOSTER

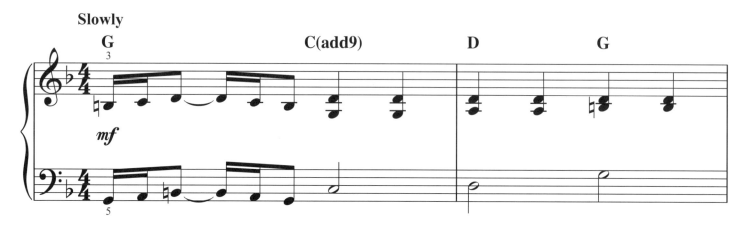

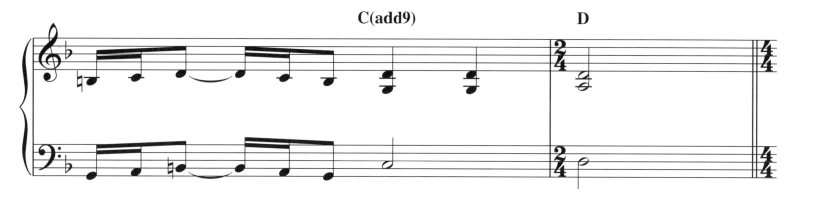

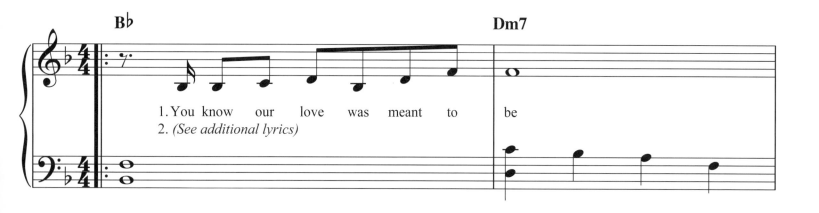

1. You know our love was meant to be
2. *(See additional lyrics)*

the kind of love that lasts __ for - ev - er. _____

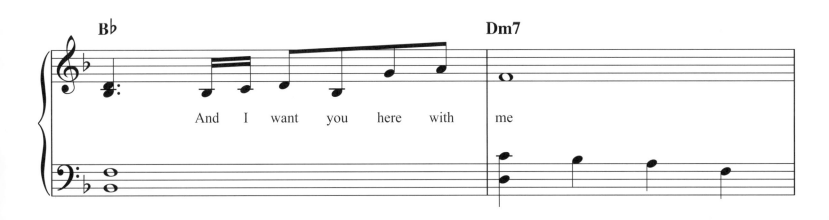

And I want you here with me

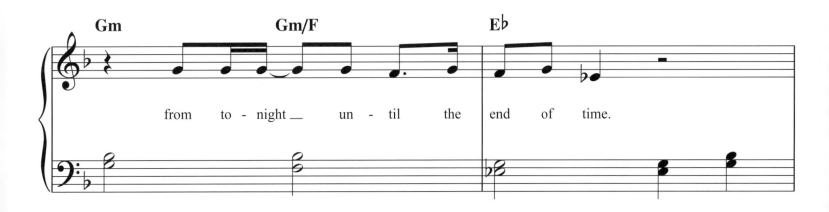

from to - night __ un - til the end of time.

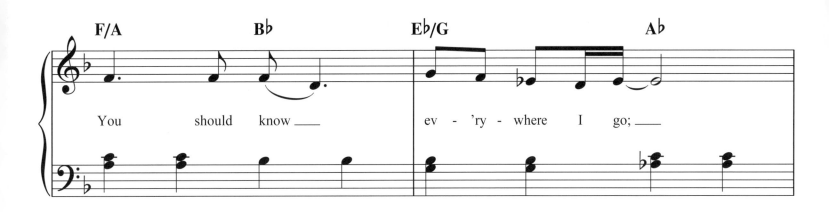

You should know ___ ev - 'ry - where I go; ___

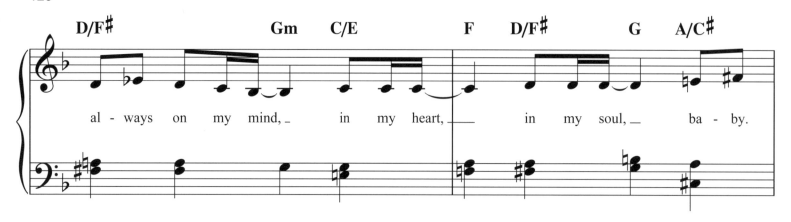

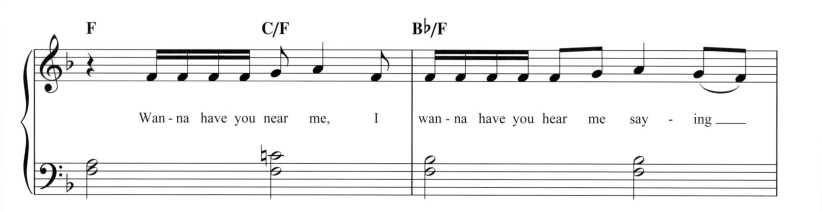

127

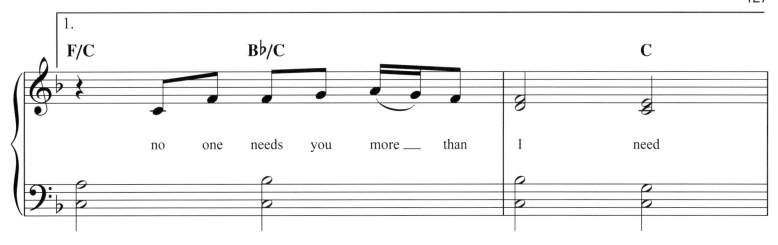

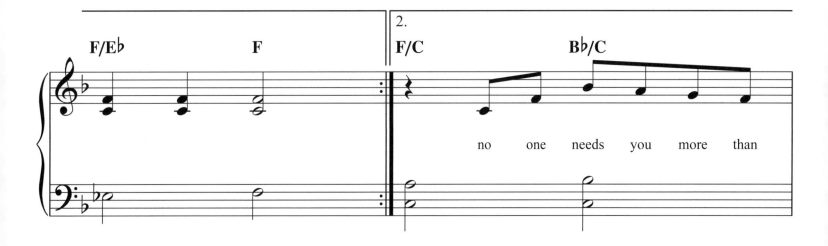

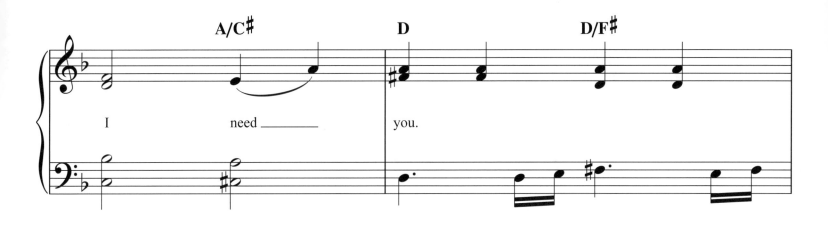

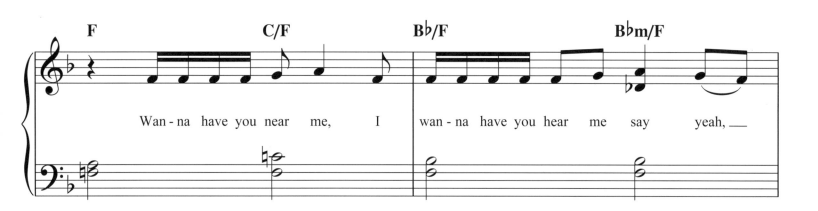

Wan - na have you near me, I wan - na have you hear me say yeah, __

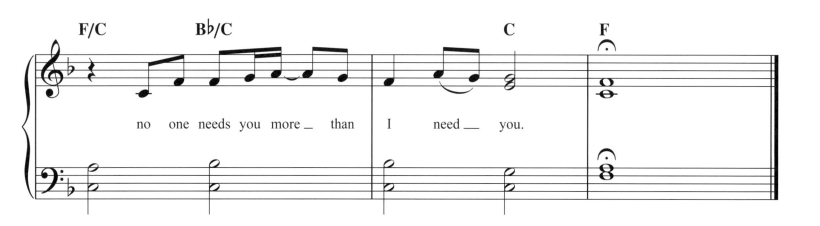

no one needs you more __ than I need __ you.

Additional Lyrics

2. And I know (yes, I know)
   That it's plain to see
   We're so in love when we're together.
   Now I know (now I know)
   That I need you here with me
   From tonight until the end of time.
   You should know, everywhere I go;
   Always on my mind, you're in my heart, in my soul.
   Chorus